Top 25-sight locator
map (continues on
inside back cover)
←

Fodor's C I T Y P A C K
brussels & bruges

by Anthony Sattin
and Sylvie Franquet

Fodor's Travel Publications
New York • Toronto •
London • Sydney • Auckland
www.fodors.com

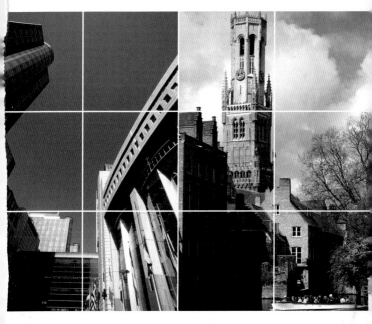

About This Book

KEY TO SYMBOLS

✚ Map reference to the fold-out
map and Top 25 locator map

✉ Address

☎ Telephone number

🕐 Opening/closing times

🍴 Restaurant or café on premises
or nearby

🚆 Nearest railway station

Ⓜ Nearest metro station

🚌 Nearest bus route

⚓ Nearest riverboat or ferry stop

♿ Facilities for visitors with
disabilities

✋ Admission charge: Expensive
(over €5), Moderate (€2.50–€5),
or Inexpensive (€2.50 or less).

↔ Other nearby places of interest

❓ Other practical information

➤ Indicates the page where you
will find a fuller description

ℹ Tourist information

ORGANIZATION
This guide is divided into six sections:
- Planning Ahead, Getting There
- Living Brussels & Bruges—Brussels & Bruges Now, Brussels & Bruges Then,
  Time to Shop, Out and About, Walks, Brussels & Bruges by Night
- Brussels' & Bruges' Top 25 Sights
- Brussels' & Bruges' Best—best of the rest
- Where To—detailed listings of restaurants, hotels, shops, and nightlife
- Travel Facts—packed with practical information

In addition, easy-to-read side panels provide extra facts and snippets,
highlights of places to visit, and invaluable practical advice.

The colours of the tabs on the page corners match the colours of the triangles
aligned with the chapter names on the contents page opposite.

MAPS
The fold-out map in the wallet at the back of this book has a comprehensive
street plan of Brussels with an inset of Bruges. The first (or only) map
reference given for each attraction refers to this map. **The Top 25 locator
maps** found on the inside front (Brussels) and back (Bruges) covers of the
book itself are for quick reference. They show the Top 25 Sights, described
on pages 26–50, which are clearly plotted by number (**1** – **25**, not page
number) across the cities. The second map reference given for the Top 25
Sights refers to these maps.

Contents

Planning Ahead

WHEN TO GO

Belgium has warm summers and mild winters. Temperatures pick up around Easter, and more attractions open. The country's northern location gives it gloriously long summer nights, perfect for sitting at outdoor cafés. The peak tourist season is July and August, when the crowds add to the buzz in Brussels but can overwhelm Bruges.

TIME

Belgium is one hour ahead of GMT, 6 hours ahead of New York, and 9 hours ahead of Los Angeles.

AVERAGE DAILY TEMPERATURES

JAN	FEB	MAR	APR	MAY	JUN	JUL	AUG	SEP	OCT	NOV	DEC
5°C	6°C	9°C	11°C	15°C	18°C	20°C	20°C	19°C	15°C	10°C	6°C
41°F	43°F	48°F	52°F	59°F	64°F	68°F	68°F	66°F	59°F	50°F	43°F

Spring (April to May) may take a while to arrive, but by May the weather is warmer and sunnier.
Summer (June to August) can be glorious—or cloudy and rainy.
Autumn (September to November) sees mild temperatures, and there can be good, clear days, especially in September and October.
Winter (December to March) has little snow and the temperatures rarely get below freezing, but it rains frequently, sometimes accompanied by strong winds and hail.

WHAT'S ON

January *Brussels International Film Festival.* www.brusselsfestival.be
April–May Brussels' royal greenhouses (Serres Royales) open to the public (➤ 57).
May *Procession of the Holy Blood* in Bruges (➤ 62). *Brussels Jazz Marathon* (end of May): Concerts on Grand' Place and in 60 bars (www.brusselsjazzmarathon.be). *Brussels Half Marathon* (20km/12.5 miles) ☎ 02 511 9000; www.sibp.be/20km. *Summer Festival* (May/ Jun–Sep): Classical concerts in Brussels.

June Re-enactment of the Battle of Waterloo at Waterloo (mid-Jun, every five years; next event due 2006) ☎ 02 354 9910.
July *Brussels Ommegang* (first Thu, ➤ 62). *Cactus Festival* in Bruges (second weekend). Open-air concerts in Minnewater Park, Bruges. *Foire du Midi* (mid-Jul to mid-Aug): Largest fair in Europe, in Brussels. *National Day* (21 Jul): Festivities in Brussels.
August Raising of the *Meiboom*, or maypole, in Brussels (9 Aug, ➤ 62). *Floral carpet* (mid-Aug, even-numbered years): On Brussels' Grand' Place. *Reiefeesten* or Festival of the Canals (every three years; next in 2005) in Bruges.
August–September *Gouden Boomstoet* or Pageant of the Golden Tree (every five years, ➤ 62) in Bruges. *Heritage Days*: Hundreds of houses and monuments open to the public across Belgium.
October–December *Europalia*: Arts and cultural events in Brussels.

BRUSSELS & BRUGES ONLINE

www.belgianstyle.com
This site includes a guide to Belgian beers, with a description of the different varieties, where they are brewed and sold, the special glasses that go with them, and, of course, a list of the best bars.

www.brugge.be
This site is run by the Tourist Office in Bruges and has practical information, virtual walks through the city, history, basics, and recommendations for hotels, restaurants, and excursions.

www.brusselsdiscovery.com
The website of the Brussels Tourist Office has plenty of suggestions on how to discover the city over a weekend. Lots of practical information, a few quirky ideas, inexpensive hotel deals, and a virtual comic-strip walk—it's all easy to find.

www.frites.be
Comic but flippant webzine in French covering everything Belgian.

www.modobruxellae.be
Modo Bruxellae runs Belgian fashion shows and loves all that is design. Every year it organizes a Designers' Trail through Brussels. The site has details of Belgian designers and designer sales.

www.noctis.com
Listings of bars, clubs, parties, music events, and festivals, as well as information for gay travellers.

www.tintin.be
Everything you ever wanted to know about Tintin, Belgium's comic strip hero.

www.toerismevlaanderen.be
This excellent website, run by the Tourism Flanders office in Brussels, offers information on Bruges, Brussels, and the rest of Flanders. It gives a bird's eye view of the region, information on events, art collections, and accommodation, and links to other websites.

GOOD TRAVEL SITES

www.fodors.com
A complete travel-planning site. You can research prices and weather; book air tickets, cars, and rooms; ask questions (and get answers) from fellow travellers; and find links to other sites.

www.trabel.com
The award-winning site of Belgium Travel Network has general information about Belgium, but specializes in practical information on car rental, travel, airlines, and hotels. It also has a shop with Belgian products.

CYBERCAFÉS

Avenue Cyber Theatre
✚ F8 ✉ 4–5 avenue de la Toison d'Or, Brussels ☎ 02 500 7878 🕐 Mon–Sat 10AM–11PM 💶 €6.20 per hour (€2.48 with a Cybercard).

Cyberb@r
✚ E7 ✉ place de Brouckère, Brussels ☎ 02 211 0820; www.easyeverything.com 🕐 24 hours 🚇 De Brouckère 💶 €1.50–2.50 per hour.

Cybercafé DNA
✚ cIII ✉ Langestraat 145, Bruges ☎ 050 34 10 93 🕐 11–9 💶 7 cents per minute (minimum charge €1.24).

5

Getting There

INSURANCE

EU nationals receive medical treatment with form E111—obtain this form before travelling. Full health and travel insurance is still advised. US travellers should check their health coverage before departure. Full insurance is advised for all other travellers.

MONEY

The euro (€) is the official currency of Belgium. Notes in denominations of 5, 10, 20, 50, 100, 200, and 500 euros, and coins in denominations of 1, 2, 5, 10, 20, and 50 cents, and 1 and 2 euros, were introduced in 2002.

€10

€50

€200

€500

ARRIVING

The international airport is Zaventem, 14km (9 miles) northeast of Brussels. Eurostar trains from London Waterloo arrive at Brussels' Gare du Midi station. Car ferries and jetfoils arrive at the ports of Zeebrugge and Oostende.

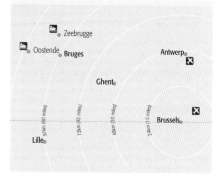

Zeebrugge

Oostende Bruges

Antwerp

Ghent

97 km (60 miles)

72 km (45 miles)

48 km (30 miles)

24 km (15 miles)

Brussels

Lille

ARRIVING BY AIR

For information on Zaventem airport (also known as Brussels Airport) ☎ 02 753 3913 (🕐 7AM–10PM); www.brusselsairport.com.

The Airport City Express shuttle train takes passengers from the airport to Brussels' main railway stations every 15–20 minutes (🕐 5.15AM–11.45PM; journey time 30 minutes; cost €2.40). For 24-hour information ☎ 02 753 2440.

De Lijn buses (☎ 016 31 37 37) to Brussels' Gare du Nord/Noordstation leave from the second-floor level of the airport's new terminal, hourly (🕐 6AM–midnight; journey time 35 minutes; cost €2).

Regular trains leave for Bruges from Brussels' South, North, and Central stations (☎ 02 555 2525; journey time one hour; cost €10.30). Trains run 4.30AM–11PM weekdays, less frequently weekends.

Taxis outside the airport's arrivals hall display a blue-and-yellow emblem, but they are expensive (around €25 to Brussels). Many accept credit cards; confirm with the driver before you travel.

ARRIVING BY TRAIN

Eurostar trains from London arrive at Brussels' Gare du Midi (journey time 2 hours 40 minutes; www.eurostar.com). Trains to Bruges leave from the same station (► 6). The TGV from Paris also arrives at Gare du Midi. Trains connect many major European cities to Brussels, and there are trains from Germany and Holland to Bruges.

ARRIVING BY SEA

Hoverspeed's Seacat Catamaran sails from Dover, in the UK, to Oostende (☎ 0870 240 8070; www.hoverspeed.com; journey time 2 hours). To drive from Oostende to Bruges and Brussels take the A10/E40 (20 minutes to Bruges; 70 minutes to Brussels).

P&O North Sea Ferries sail overnight from Hull, in the UK, to Zeebrugge (www.ponsf.com; journey time 14 hours). To drive to Bruges take the N31 and N371 (15 minutes); to Brussels take the N31 and E40 (1 hour 15 minutes).

There are rail links from Oostende and Zeebrugge (90 minutes to Brussels; 30 minutes to Bruges). Ferries from Dover to the French port of Calais take 75 minutes; Hoverspeed's Seacat takes 50 minutes. To drive from Calais to Bruges take the E40 (1 hour 20 minutes); from Calais to Brussels take the E15/E40 (2 hours).

ARRIVING BY BUS

Eurolines buses connect major European cities with Brussels (www.eurolines.com). The international bus station is CCN Gare du Nord/Noordstation (✉ 80 rue du Progrès ☎ 02 203 0707). There are frequent trains from Gare du Nord to Bruges (► 6).

GETTING AROUND

Brussels has trams, buses, and metro trains. Metro stations are indicated by a white letter "M." A ticket is valid for 1 hour and must be stamped on the bus or tram or in the metro station. Use only official taxis, with a taxi light on the roof. Bruges has an efficient bus network, although it is easy to walk everywhere. A one-day bus pass (*dagticket*) is available.

For more advice on getting around ► 91–92.

ENTRY REQUIREMENTS

EU citizens need a national identity card or passport for visits of up to three months.
Visitors from the US, Japan, Canada, Australia, and New Zealand need a valid passport for visits of up to three months.
Your passport should be valid for at least 6 months.

VISITORS WITH DISABILITIES

There are few facilities on buses, trams, and the metro for people with disabilities, but a minibus service equipped for wheelchairs is available at low cost from the public transport network STIB/MIVB (☎ 02 515 2365). On trains outside Brussels, a passenger accompanying a passenger with disabilities travels free.

Few buildings in Brussels and Bruges have facilities for people with disabilities, and the streets have uneven cobblestones, which are tough on wheelchairs. For more information contact Mobility International (✉ boulevard Baudouin 18 ☎ 02 201 5608; fax 02 201 5763).

Living
Brussels & Bruges

Brussels & Bruges Now

Above: *canal trips are a popular way of exploring Bruges*

Contrasting Cities

Brussels and Bruges represent the twin identity of modern Belgium. Brussels is the larger, busier, and more commercially orientated city—it is also Belgium's political capital (and Europe's). Bruges is Belgium's tourist capital and is one of Europe's best-preserved medieval cities. Culturally the cities are divided by their roots— Flemish-speaking Bruges is in Flanders, while Brussels borders predominantly French-speaking Walloonia. Rivalry endures between those who speak Flemish and those who speak French.

BRUSSELS' DISTRICTS

• The heart of Brussels is relatively small, enclosed by what is called the *petit ring*, which in turn more or less follows the 14th-century city walls. It has two halves: the Lower Town, where the lower-middle and working classes lived near the Grand' Place, and the Upper Town, on the hill where the French-speaking upper classes and the royal family lived. Much of the old Lower Town was destroyed during a French bombardment in 1695, except for the St. Catherine area, with its cobbled streets, fish restaurants, and lively night scene. The Upper Town is totally different, with grand buildings around the Sablon, the palace, and the Musées des Beaux Arts. To the east is the Quartier Léopold, where mansions had to make way for the steel and concrete of the EU quarter, where European Union officials work. South are the trendy districts of Ixelles and St. Gilles.

Left: *the modern exteriors of Brussels' EU quarter*
Below: *an outside café is the perfect place to relax in summer*

Vibrant Brussels

Brussels has many attractions for the day and a more-than-energetic nightlife. At its heart is one of Europe's most beautiful squares, the Grand' Place, famous for its stunning medieval guild houses and Gothic town hall.

True, Brussels is not the easiest place to get to know—it has a reputation as a city full of bureaucrats, who work in one of the many offices of the European Parliament or NATO. But with a little effort you can discover its many pleasures—its gastronomic delights, the quirky little museums, the pleasurable green areas, the splendid art nouveau architecture, and an impressive variety of watering holes. Perhaps most difficult of all is to learn something about the Belgians themselves, who can be reserved unless you catch them after a few pints of the local brew. And when you do meet them, which language do you speak? Most speak French but there is also an important Flemish-speaking community. More and more often—and perhaps as a result of Brussels' status as an international centre—the lingua franca is English. Flemings (Flemish-speakers) and

CITY OF BRIDGES

No name is more appropriate than *Brugge*, Flemish for bridge. The city had its origins around a bridge over the canal (*reie*), probably the Blind Donkey bridge. To protect the crossing, a borough was built and the city grew around it. Bruges still has about 80 bridges, the newest commissioned to celebrate Bruges' designation as European City of Culture in 2002.

THE ROYAL FAMILY

• The Belgian monarchy goes back some 160 years. The Belgian king, Albert II, like the British monarch today, is a constitutional head of state who wields little real power but can exert some influence on the government. The current heir, Prince Philippe, won the hearts of the nation by marrying Princesse Mathilde. After the birth of their first daughter, Princess Elisabeth, in 2000, the constitution was changed to allow a woman to become head of state.

Walloons (French-speakers) do mix in bars and restaurants, but they tend to congregate separately in certain areas: Ixelles, for instance, is more French, while the centre and the area around the rue Dansaert is more Flemish. There is an up side to this division: You get twice as much cultural life to choose from.

During the past decade or so great efforts have been made to restore Brussels' historic buildings. The Grand' Place has survived the centuries remarkably well, as have other pockets of historic Brussels, like the Sablon area. But elsewhere, the city has suffered from neglect and greedy property speculation—first-time visitors are sometimes surprised at the state of decay in parts of the centre. Following World War II, many Bruxellois/Brusselaars moved out of the centre to the greener suburbs, leaving the historic core to the city's poor and to property speculators, who pulled down many great old buildings to provide massive new buildings for international agencies. This neglect is now being reversed and the authorities are trying hard to make the heart of the city attractive again.

Above: *a game of boules in the parc de Bruxelles*
Left: *a view of Bruges' Markt from the top of the Belfry*
Far left: *the elegant shopping arcade Galeries St.-Hubert*

Bruges: Medieval meets modern

Bruges attracts more visitors than any other Belgian city, including Brussels, and it is not difficult to understand why. It is an easy city to get around, with most of its sights within walking distance of one another. Its art and architecture are truly wonderful. For many years now, Bruges and its people have thrived off this

TO BE BELGIAN

- It is often said that there are no longer any Belgians, only Flemings, Walloons, and Bruxellois, but things are not that simple. The nation is deeply divided over historical and political issues, but the three communities have much in common. Although the Belgians are probably the least nationalistic people in the world, many Belgians seem drawn to the concept of being Belgian: Car stickers announcing "I'm Belgian and I'm proud of it" in the two languages are common, as are bilingual marriages and friendships. And every so often artists and film makers from both sides celebrate, with typically dry Belgian humour, the surrealism and absurdity of having such a mix of people and languages in this tiny country.

REVOLUTIONARY OPERA

- On 25 August 1830, provoked by the opera *La Muette*, the elegant audience stormed out of the Théâtre de la Monnaie and joined a workers' demonstration outside. Together they stormed the Palais de Justice and drove out the Dutch rulers. This was the beginning of the Belgian revolution.

Above: *admiring the fountain in avenue de Tervuren*
Right: *flower market in the Grand' Place*
Far right: *a stunning view of Bruges from the roof-top café at the Concertgebouw*

medieval heritage and in this city, unlike Brussels, everything has been done to keep the overall look as medieval as possible. Many people regard the success of this policy as a mixed blessing and some would like to see Bruges more accurately reflect the tastes of those who live in it now. They have raised fears about the city becoming a victim of its own popularity and have mocked the strict

EQUAL RIGHTS

• It's not just language that divides Belgians into their regions—there are regional parliaments as well as the national parliament. Great efforts are made by the central government to avoid showing partiality, often with absurd results: When money was allocated for roads in the northern region of Flanders, for instance, the southern region of Walloonia received identical funding, even though this resulted in one highway ending in the middle of a field.

regulations that have ensured the city's survival, joking that they will soon be asked to dress up in medieval costume during the tourist season.

But something is happening in Bruges. Its selection as European City of Culture in 2002 has finally made the city look towards the future. The past will always hover and will certainly not easily be forgotten, but the city council has made a brave decision to ignore dissent and commission important contemporary architects and artists to give the place a new look and feel. The main project was the new Concertgebouw, which offers a large space with the best concert facilities in the country and should ensure a prime cultural position for Bruges within Belgium. Long ago, the Flemish Primitives thrived in Bruges. Now there is a desire to create an ambience in which local and international contemporary artists will be inspired both by the modern city and by its rich past.

VITAL STATISTICS

● Nearly 80 percent of Bruxellois are French-speakers; 20 percent are Flemish-speakers.

● Brussels is the world's second-greenest capital, with 13.8 percent of the city being green space.

● Bruges is Belgium's No. 1 tourist destination, attracting more than 2.5 million visitors each year.

● More than 150 monuments in Bruges have been protected.

15

Brussels & Bruges Then

EARLY DAYS

Brocsella (Brussels) was first mentioned in AD 695 on the trade route between Cologne and Flanders.

In 979 Charles, Duke of Lorraine, moved to St.-Géry (central Brussels), founding the city.

In 1459 Philip the Good, having inherited Flanders and Burgundy, brought Brabant and Holland under his control and settled in Brussels.

A GREAT KING

Although Belgium is a democracy led by a prime minister, King Baudouin I, who died in 1993, did much to unify the country. He made a stand on matters where his principles were at stake: During the 1990 abortion debate he found himself unable to sign the law so he abdicated for a day to allow it to be passed.

BRUSSELS

1515 Charles V, soon to be Holy Roman Emperor and King of Spain and the Netherlands, arrives in the city and stays until he abdicates in 1555.

1568 A revolt begins that leads to the independence of the United Province of the Netherlands from Spain, but not of present-day Belgium, which becomes known as the Spanish Netherlands.

1695 French forces attack Brussels, destroying 4,000 buildings.

1713–94 Brussels is capital of the Austrian Netherlands, under Hapsburg rule.

1795 Brussels is under French rule.

1815 Brussels reverts to the Dutch, after Napoleon Bonaparte's defeat at the Battle of Waterloo.

1830 The Belgian Revolution leads to independence in January 1831.

1957 Brussels becomes the HQ of the EEC, and 10 years later the HQ of NATO.

1993 Belgium becomes a federal state.

2002 Euro notes and coins are introduced.

BRUGES

c300 AD Bryggja is established, named for a key bridge.

1127 The first walls go up around Bruges.

1302 Flemish craftsmen and peasants defeat a French army at the Battle of the Golden Spurs.

1468 Charles the Bold, Duke of Burgundy and son of Philip the Good, marries Margaret of York in Damme.

1488 An uprising against Archduke Maximilian, the Hapsburg heir who tried to limit the city's privileges, leads to his kidnap and three months' detention in Bruges. The reprisals against the Bruges burghers begin the steady decline of the city when Maximilian becomes emperor in 1493.

1898 Flemish is officially recognized as the country's joint language with French.

1907 New Boudewijn Canal links Bruges again with the port of Zeebrugge, creating industrial development.

2002 The opening of the Concertgebouw puts Bruges at the forefront of Flanders' cultural life.

Left to right: the Duke of Wellington attends a ball in Brussels on the eve of the Battle of Waterloo, 1815; Grand' Place, c1895; Bruges town plan, c1572; a canal in Bruges, c1900

TRADING SUCCESS

By the early 14th century Bruges had become one of the world's great trading cities. In 1384 Philip the Bold, Duke of Burgundy, inherited Flanders and ushered in a period of prosperity and great cultural and political changes. However, the city began to decline when Maximilian became emperor in 1493. In 1516 Genoese and Florentine traders, who had set up business ventures in Bruges under a treaty of 1395, moved to Antwerp. A further difficulty arose in 1550, when Bruges lost access to the sea, with the silting up of what is now known as the Zwin.

Time to Shop

Below: *Belgium is famous for its handmade chocolates*
Right: *cheese and meats fill the counter in the old-fashioned interior of the Diksmuids Boterhuis*

An obvious souvenir from Belgium, if not a lasting one, is food. Belgium is renowned for its high quality plain chocolate, which uses only the best cocoa and a very high proportion of it (between 52 and 90 percent). Belgians are serious about their chocolate, as is obvious from

SHOPPING DISTRICTS

Brussels has two main shopping areas: the city centre around the Grand' Place, and Ixelles, to the south. The main shopping street, rue Neuve, is lined with stores of many international chains, as is the large shopping mall City2. The area around the rue Dansaert is home to many Belgian designers, while more conservative shops, selling anything from cutlery and gloves to chocolates and books, can be found in the wonderful Galeries St.-Hubert.
In Bruges the two main shopping streets are the Geldmuntstraat (and its continuation Noord-zandstraat) and the Steenstraat-Zuidzandstraat.

the number of shops devoted to chocolate in its many, many shapes, shades, and flavours. You can buy good chocolate bars, such as Callebaut or Côte d'Or, in supermarkets, but it's the handmade chocolates and pralines that stand out. Prices are generally low, except for chocolate by Pierre Marcolino and by the internationally renowned Godiva, and the fillings are delightful, particularly those using fresh cream. Do as the Belgians and look for smaller *patisseries* that make their own, including Speghelaere and Depla in Bruges and Mary in Brussels.

After you've sampled the chocolate, try a Belgian waffle, eaten with powdered sugar or whipped cream, or *speculoos* (slightly spicy biscuits). Also popular are *pain Grècque* (a light biscuit with sugar), *amandelbrood* (butter biscuit with shaved almonds), and *peperkoek* (a cake with cinnamon and candied fruits). Destrooper is a good brand and is stocked in supermarkets.

Beer is another good buy, with 700 labels to choose from. Every bar has a beer menu, so you might want to try a few varieties before stocking up. Larger supermarkets have a good selection of beers, and beer shops can be found in tourist areas in both cities.

Below left: *cutting-edge fashion at the Stijl shop on rue Antoine Dansaert*
Below: *Belgian beer*

Belgium was famous in the Middle Ages for its tapestry and exquisite lace, and there is still plenty of it for sale, although very little is now handmade in Belgium and what you can find is usually very pricey. Belgian fashion designers are currently enjoying worldwide success, so take a closer look at their work in Brussels, particularly in and around the rue Dansaert. Local designers such as Dries Van Noten, Martin Margiela, and Veronique Branquinho create innovative designs based on Belgian traditions.

Art galleries are all over Brussels—for details obtain a copy of the brochure *Art Brussels* from the tourist office. Many shops specialize in comic books and paraphernalia related to comic strips, but none so much as the Tintin shops in both cities. Here you can buy the books, collectables, clothes, towels, and even wallpaper bearing the image of Tintin, the celebrated Belgian comic strip hero.

THE WISE ST. ARNOLD

Belgian beer is famously good and it comes as no surprise that there is a patron saint of brewers. The story goes that in the 11th century, when the plague raged through Belgium, a Benedictine monk dipped his crucifix in the big brewer's kettle. This was done to encourage Belgians to drink beer instead of the plague-infested water. And guess what? The plague stopped and the monk was beatified soon after as St. Arnold.

19

Out and About

INFORMATION

Pro Vélo
Explore Brussels by bike.
☎ 02 502 7355;
www.provelo.org
**ARAU *Brussels 1900*
bus tours**
Art nouveau architecture.
✉ 55 boulevard Adolphe
Max ☎ 02 219 3345;
www.arau.org
🕘 Mar–Nov: Sat
Brussels City Tours
✉ 8 De Boeck, rue de la
Colline ☎ 02 513 7744;
www.brussels-city-
tours.com
Chatterbus Tours
✉ 12 rue des Thuyas,
Brussels ☎ 02 673 1835;
www.busbavard.be
Bruges by Boat
✉ From Katelijnestraat,
Wollestraat, Vismarkt, the
Dijver, Huidenvettersplein
🕘 Mar–Nov: 10–6.
Dec weekends only
Bruges by Bike Quasimodo
☎ 0800 97525; www.
quasimodo.be 🕘 10AM
City Tour Brugge
☎ 050 35 50 24

INFORMATION

LEUVEN
Distance 19km (12 miles)
from Brussels
Journey Time 15 minutes
🚆 Frequent trains from
the Gare Centrale, Gare du
Nord, or Gare du Midi
🛈 9 Grote Markt
(☎ 016 21 15 39)

ORGANIZED SIGHTSEEING

The old-fashioned way to tour Brussels is by horse-drawn cab from the rue Charles Buls, near the Grand' Place (☎ 053 70 05 04 🕘 Daily in summer; on dry weekends in winter). A number of groups offer bus and walking tours, focusing

on the city's main attractions or on particular themes, such as art nouveau architecture or sights associated with comic strips.

In Bruges, Bruges by Boat offers canal trips, and Bruges by Bike Quasimodo gives guided bicycle tours. A coach from City Tour Brugge leaves the Markt hourly for a 50-minute tour of Bruges' historic sights.

EXCURSIONS
LEUVEN

Leuven is a pleasant Flemish university town, with a handful of striking buildings. The 15th-century Stadhuis (town hall) on the Grote Markt is typical of late Brabant Gothic style, while the Tafelrond is a neo-Gothic reconstruction of 15th-century houses. St. Peter's Church has two triptychs by the 15th-century painter Dirk Bouts. The grandest of all the cafés around the Grote Markt is Café Gambrinus, which has pre-art nouveau frescoes. Nearby is St.-Michielskerk, a marvel of 17th-century baroque, while the Groot Begijnhof is a village in itself, with 17th- and 18th-century houses, now part of Belgium's largest university, the Catholic University of Leuven.

WATERLOO

Here is the famous battlefield where the Duke of Wellington defeated Napoleon Bonaparte on 18 June 1815. Most people come to see the Butte de Lion, a grass-covered pyramid marking the spot where William of Orange was wounded. At the

foot of the mound is the visitor centre with a Waterloo panorama. It is worth climbing the 226 steps for the views from the top. The Wellington Museum, in the inn where the Duke lodged, shows memorabilia from the battle. So does the Museum of Caillou, on a farm where Napoleon spent the night.

DAMME

When the old port in Bruges dried out after the estuary silted up, the focus of trade shifted to the small town of Damme. Today it is a popular excursion along the canal by foot, bicycle, or boat, with culinary delights at the end: Restaurants offer local fare such as Damme tart, Damme sausages, a semi-hard Damme cheese, and *anguilles au vert* (river eel in herb sauce). On the main square is the 19th-century statue of the Flemish poet Jacob van Maerlant (1235–1300). The elegant Gothic Stadhuis (Town Hall) of 1464 has two punishment stones on the corner and some fine mouldings inside the Council Hall and the Vierschaere. There are magnificent views from the tower of the 14th-century Church of Our Lady.

INFORMATION

WATERLOO
Distance 20km (12.5 miles) from Brussels
Journey Time 15 minutes
🚆 Frequent trains from the main stations. The station is 1km (0.6 miles) from the heart of Waterloo but you can rent bicycles at the next station, Braine-l'Alleud, under the Train et Vélo scheme.
🛈 Tourist Office (✉ chaussée de Bruxelles 149, Braine-l'Alleud ☎ 02 385 1912)
Wellington Museum ☎ 02 354 7806
Museum of Caillou ☎ 02 384 2424
Visitor Centre ✉ route du Lion 252 ☎ 02 385 1912

Left to right: *the facade of Leuven's Stadhuis; the canal at Damme; silhouette of the Butte de Lion*

INFORMATION

DAMME
Distance 6.5km (4 miles) from Bruges
Journey Time Bus 15 minutes; boat 35 minutes
🚌 4 from Markt (signposted for Koolkerke)
🚤 *Lamme Goedzak* runs Apr–Sep (✉ Noorweegse Kaai 31 ☎ 050 35 33 19)
🛈 Huyse de Grote Sterre, Jakob van Maerlanstraat 3 (☎ 050 35 33 19)

Walks

INFORMATION

Distance 1.5km (1 mile)
Time 1–2 hours
Start point
★ Grand' Place
🚇 E7
🚉 Gare Centrale/
Centraal Station or
Bourse/Beurs
🚊 Tram 23, 52, 55, 56, 81
End point rue des
Bouchers
🚇 E7

THE CRADLE OF BRUSSELS, FROM MANNEKEN TO JANNEKEN PIS

Leave the Grand' Place (➤ 30) via rue Charles Buls. Walk along rue de l'Etuve, leading to Manneken Pis (➤ 31), then turn right onto rue Grands-Carmes to the rue Marché du Charbon. Walk past Église Notre-Dame du Bon-Secours to boulevard Anspach. Turn right onto the boulevard and then left onto rue des Riches Claires, with a 17th-century church. Turn right onto rue de la Grande Île, where, immediately left, a passageway leads to the back of the church and the original site of the River Senne.

Return to place St.-Géry where a plaque on a 19th-century covered market indicates the site of Brussels' origins. Walk along rue du Pont de la Carpe and then left onto rue Antoine Dansaert, where there are restaurants and clothes shops. Take a right onto rue du Vieux Marché aux Grains, leading to place Ste.-Catherine, built on the basin of Brussels' old port, which explains why there is still a fish market and fish restaurants. Walk past the Tour Noire, part of the first city wall, back to boulevard Anspach, and cross over onto rue de l'Evêque to place de la Monnaie, with the Théâtre de la Monnaie. Take a right onto rue des Fripiers and left onto rue Grétry, which becomes rue des Bouchers, where Janneken Pis (➤ 31) is signposted.

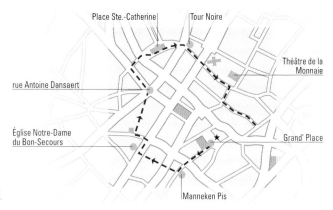

Place Ste.-Catherine Tour Noire

Théâtre de la Monnaie

rue Antoine Dansaert

Église Notre-Dame du Bon-Secours

Grand' Place

Manneken Pis

LESSER-KNOWN BRUGES

Start at the Boomgaardstraat, with the baroque church of St. Walburga (➤ 55). Turn right onto the Hoornstraat and then right on Verwersdijk. Cross over the bridge and walk along St.-Annakerkstraat to the Jeruzalemstraat with the Jeruzalemkerk (➤ 55) to the right. Next door is the Kantcentrum (➤ 72), where you can see how lace is made.

Walk along Balstraat, with the Museum voor Volkskunde (➤ 53). Cross Rolweg to Carmersstraat and turn right. No. 85 is the English convent; No. 174 is the old Schuttersgilde St.-Sebastiaan, the archers' guildhouse; and straight ahead on Kruisvest is the St.-Janshuys windmill (➤ 57). Take a right along Kruisvest. On the corner with Rolweg is a museum dedicated to the Flemish poet Guido Gezelle (1830–99) and farther along, the Bonne Chiere windmill. At the Kruispoort, turn right onto Langestraat. At No. 47 is the Brewery Museum (☎ 050 33 06 99 ✆ May–Sep: Wed– Sun 2–6). Before the end of Langestraat, turn left onto Predikherenstraat, just past the bridge and turn right to Groenerei, one of Bruges' loveliest corners. At the end of the street is Vismarkt, with a fish market (Tuesday to Saturday mornings). To the right an alley under the arch leads to the Burg (➤ 49).

INFORMATION

Distance 2km (1.2 miles)
Time 2 hours
Start point
★ St.-Walburgakerk
✚ cIII
🚌 6
End point Burg
✚ bIII
🚌 1, 2, 3, 4, 8, 11, 13, 17

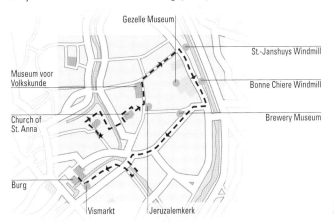

Gezelle Museum

St.-Janshuys Windmill

Museum voor Volkskunde

Bonne Chiere Windmill

Church of St. Anna

Brewery Museum

Burg

Vismarkt

Jeruzalemkerk

Brussels & Bruges by Night

Left: *inside Le Falstaff bar*
Right: *a view of the Belfry, from the Eiermarkt, Bruges*

WHAT'S ON

Brussels' daily newspapers have listings. The English-language weekly *The Bulletin* has a "What's On" supplement. *Humo* has listings in Flemish, and *Kiosk* covers nightlife, concerts, and exhibitions in French.
Tickets are usually available at the venues, but can also be purchased from Tourist Information Brussels (✉ Grand' Place ☎ 02 513 8940) or FNAC bookshop and ticket agency (✉ City2 rue Neuve ☎ 02 209 2211). In Bruges, the monthly *Exit* magazine, available free at the tourist office, includes a calendar of events.

THE BAR SCENE

The Belgian joke that there's a bar on every corner can't be far from the truth. What's more, these bars or cafés are rarely empty and licensing laws permit them to stay open as long as they like—often until dawn. The bar scene is very lively in both cities, as this is what locals do when they go out at night. Even if they go out for dinner or to the theatre, they still end up having a beer in a bar. The pace of drinking is usually steady but slow, making it easier to keep going all night. In Brussels you can start on the Grand' Place, where the view comes at a price. Nearby there are trendy bars around the place St.-Géry and rue Marché au Charbon, as well as pricier establishments around Le Sablon. Look in Les Marolles for distinctively Bruxellois cafés, stained dark from decades of tobacco smoke. For cosmopolitan jazz clubs and wine bars, try Ixelles.

AN EVENING STROLL

Head for the Grand' Place, beautifully floodlit at night, and to the rue des Bouchers with its many restaurants, most attracting tourists. In Bruges, the liveliest areas are the Eiermarkt and t'Zandt.

OUTDOOR LIVING

In summer, Belgians spend long evenings sitting on café terraces chatting with friends. The best terraces in Brussels include Le Roy d'Espagne, La Lunette, Le Falstaff (all ➤ 70), and the many café terraces on the place du Grand Sablon. In Bruges, most people head for cafés in the Eiermarkt and t'Zandt, as well as Bistro du Phare and l'Estaminet (both ➤ 71).

BRUSSELS' & BRUGES'
top 25 sights

The sights are shown on the maps on the inside covers, numbered **1**–**15** north to south in Brussels and **16**–**25** west to east across Bruges

Heysel

HIGHLIGHTS

- The Atomium
- Japanese Tower
- Chinese Pavilion

INFORMATION

Atomium

- ➕ D2; locator map A–B1
- ✉ boulevard du Centenaire
- ☎ 02 474 8977;
  www.atomium.be
- 🕐 Apr–Aug: daily 9–7.30.
  Sep–Mar: daily 10–5.30.
  Closed hols
- 🍴 Salon '58 (££)
  🕐 Mon–Fri 11AM–2AM;
  Sat, Sun 11AM–3AM
- 🚌 84, 89; tram 23, 81
- 🎫 Moderate
- Ⓜ Heysel/Heizel
- ♿ None

**Japanese Tower &
Chinese Pavilion**

- ➕ F2; locator map B1
- ✉ 44 avenue van Praet
- 🕐 Tue–Sun 10–4.30.
  Closed hols
- 🚌 53; tram 19, 23, 52
- 🎫 Moderate
- ♿ None

To celebrate Belgium's 100th birthday in 1930, Heysel Park was named as the site of the Centenary Stadium and the Palais du Centenaire. It was the setting of the World Exhibition of 1958, and still contains the most memorable of all the pavilions, the Atomium.

The Atomium The Atomium was designed in steel and aluminium for Expo '58 by Andre Waterkeyn. Its nine balls represent the atoms of a metal crystal enlarged 165 billion times. The building remains an extraordinary sight, symbolizing the optimism of its time. It was built to last a year, but because it became a Brussels landmark and a symbol for Belgium it is still there, currently undergoing repairs. It is used for temporary exhibitions and the panoramic view from the top of the atoms is spectacular. In a nearby pavilion is Salon '58, a trendy restaurant-bar, decorated in 1950s style. Here you can enjoy a drink or meal as well as views of the Atomium.

Stranger landmarks After the Universal Exhibition in Paris in 1900, King Leopold II wanted his own *chinoiseries*, so he commissioned Parisian architect Alexandre Marcel to create them. The striking Japanese Tower, the former Entrance Pavilion to the Japanese Pagoda from the Paris Exhibition, was brought to Brussels. The splendid Chinese Pavilion, whose facade was carved in Shanghai, houses a fine collection of porcelain from the late 17th to the early 19th centuries.

Trade space The Centenary Stadium hosts sports events and rock concerts, while the Palais de Centenaire forms the core of the Trade Mart, with ten exhibition halls.

Top: *the shining metal
orbs of the Atomium*

Centre Belge de la Bande Dessinée

"Captain Haddock: 'Land Ho! Land Ho! Thundering typhoons! Land... about time, too!' Tintin: 'Why?...Are we out of fuel-oil?' Haddock: 'Worse than that!... We're out of whisky!!'"—Hergé's *The Adventures of Tintin: The Shooting Star.*

Comic strips and more comic strips Combining comic strips and art nouveau, this is one of Brussels' unusual delights. Although comic strips, or *bds* (*bandes dessinées*), were not invented in Belgium, Belgian artists took the form to new heights. The most famous of them is Hergé (Georges Rémi), with his 1929 creations Tintin and Milou (Snowy). The wonderful collection of comic strips is housed in a stunning early-1900s building by architect Victor Horta. The Museum Bookshop stocks thousands of comic strips and collectables.

Hands-on entertainment The mezzanine houses an extensive archive, a cinema, and an exhibition explaining how *bds* are made. On the upper floor, sections are devoted to each of the great Belgian *bd* creators, with pages to admire as well as hands-on exhibits. The lower floor shows work by Victor Horta.

The Magazins Waucquez The museum is housed in a building that a merchant named Monsieur Waucquez commissioned Victor Horta to build as a fabrics shop. Opened in 1906 with plant-motif ironwork, a sweeping staircase, and glass skylight, Magazins Waucquez closed in 1970, and the building was earmarked for demolition until a pressure group and royal support saved it.

DID YOU KNOW?

- Tintin books have been translated into 51 languages
- More than 200 million Tintin books have been sold worldwide
- Brussels has a Comic Strip Frescoes Route, with the most famous characters painted on facades in the centre of Brussels (map available from tourist office on Grand' Place)
- 850 new comic strip titles are published every year in Belgium

INFORMATION

- ✚ F6–7; locator map C3
- ✉ 20 rue des Sables
- ☎ 02 219 1980
- 🕐 Tue–Sun 10–6. Closed Easter and some hols
- 🍴 Restaurant/bar
- Ⓜ Botanique/Botaniek, Gare Centrale/Centraal station, de Brouckère
- 🚌 38, 58, 61; tram 23, 52, 55, 56, 81, 90, 92, 93, 94
- ♿ Good
- 💵 Moderate
- ❓ Reading room Tue–Thu 12–5; Fri 12–6; Sat, Sun 10–6 (included in entrance fee). Library same hours, ticket moderate

Left: *Tintin's moon rocket.*
Top: *cartoon strip*   27

Cathédrale St.-Michel et Ste.-Gudule

HIGHLIGHTS

- Stained-glass windows
- 17th-century tapestries by Jaspar Van der Borght
- Nave pillars representing the 12 apostles
- Baroque pulpit by Henri Verbruggen (1699)
- Tombs of Johann of Brabant and his wife Margaret of York
- Stained glass by a pupil of Rubens in the Chapel of Our Lady of Redemption

INFORMATION

- F7; locator map C3
- parvis St.-Gudule
- 02 217 8345
- Daily 8-6
- None
- Gare Centrale/Centraal Station
- Few
- Free. Crypt inexpensive
- Grand' Place (➤ 30), place Royale (➤ 36), Centre Belge de la Bande Dessinée (➤ 27), musées d'Art Ancien et Moderne (➤ 33, 34), Musée des Instruments de Musique (➤ 35), Musée du Cinéma (➤ 84)
- Services: in French Sat 5.30, Sun 10, 11.30, 12.30; in Flemish Sat 4

Top: one of the stained-glass windows in the cathedral's nave

With its intriguing mixture of styles and influences, the cathedral of St. Michael and Ste. Gudule expresses Brussels' ability to compromise and is a fitting venue for state occasions.

Growing power During the 12th and 13th centuries, a valuable trade route between Brussels and Germany began to develop. As a result of the wealth this brought, a cathedral was planned and the splendid building was completed in the early 16th century. Subsequently embellished and added to, the building is now 108m long by 50m wide (378 feet by 164 feet), with twin towers 69m (226-foot) high. It stands on a hill between the upper and lower parts of the city. Unfortunately it is now surrounded by busy roads and ugly modern developments.

Slow start The cathedral is a mixture of middle and late Gothic styles. The earlier Romano-Gothic elements, particularly the ambulatory and choir, fit happily with those from the Late Gothic period, which are in the nave and on the west facade. Restorations undertaken since 1983 have exposed elements of an earlier Romanesque church (founded 1047) on which the cathedral was built. The original crypt is worth a visit.

Dedications Although known as St. Michael's and Ste. Gudule's, after Brussels' patron saints, and known by local people merely as Ste.-Gudule, the cathedral was officially dedicated only to St. Michael. A story tells that when the building became a cathedral, the Roman Catholic authorities admitted to knowing nothing about Gudule, an 8th-century lady of royal blood sainted for her piety, and omitted her name.

Hôtel de Ville

Had architect Jan von Ruysbroeck forseen how much his elegant bell tower for the Hôtel de Ville would be admired today, perhaps he would not have thrown himself off it.

A **Gothic masterpiece** Flanders and Brabant have a wealth of Gothic town halls, but the Brussels Hôtel de Ville is probably the most beautiful of all. It was started in the spring of 1402; the right wing was added in 1444. The octagonal tower, 96m (315 foot) high, was added later by architect Jan van Ruysbroeck and bears a gilt statue of the Archangel St. Michael. The top of the tower, 400 steps up, gives the best views over the Grand' Place and the heart of Brussels. Most sculptures adorning the facade of the Town Hall are 19th-century replacements of 14th- and 15th-century originals that are now in the Musée de la Ville de Bruxelles (▶ 53). The courtyard has two 18th-century fountains against the west wall, representing Belgium's most important rivers—the Meuse (to the left) and Scheldt (on the right).

The Grand Staircase The Grand Staircase carries the busts of all the mayors of Brussels since Belgian independence in 1830. Count Jacques Lalaing painted the murals on the walls in 1893.

The Gothic Hall The former 16th-century Council Chamber was used for official ceremonies. Its lavish 19th-century tapestries are interesting for their depiction of the city's main guilds and their crafts. The windows are decorated with the coats of arms of Brussels' guilds and noble families. Also included in the official guided tour are some of the offices of the mayors and magistrates.

Top: *town hall facade*
Above: *St. Michael*

HIGHLIGHTS

- Grand Staircase
- Bell tower
- Magnificent tapestries

INFORMATION

- ✚ E7; locator map B3
- ✉ Grand' Place
- ☎ 02 279 4365 (tourist office)
- ⊙ Guided tours only, in English; groups Thu only. During the biennial flower festival you can visit the Hôtel de Ville without a guided tour
- ⊞ Gare Centrale/Centraal Station or Bourse/Beurse
- ⊟ Tram 23, 52, 55, 56, 81
- ♿ Good
- ⊕ Moderate

29

Grand' Place

In the morning, the sun lights up the gilded Gothic, Renaissance, and baroque facades of one of the world's most stunning squares. This is the unquestionable heart of Brussels.

The centre of Brussels The Grand' Place is still the sight that all tourists come to admire. By the 11th century the marketplace was already humming, and by the 13th century organizations of tradesmen known as guilds grew up to regulate working conditions and hours as well as trading outside the town. In the 13th century the first three guildhalls, for butchers, bakers, and clothmakers, were built in the Grand' Place. From then on the guilds' power increased; they became involved in wars, including the Battle of the Golden Spurs (1302), and commanded ever higher membership fees. The guilds' might is never more palpable than when you stand in the Grand' Place. Destroyed by a French bombardment in 1695 (except for the Hôtel de Ville, ➤ 29), the square was entirely rebuilt by the guilds in less than five years.

The guildhalls Each one in the Grand' Place is distinguished by distinct statues and ornate carvings. Look for No. 5 La Louve (the She-wolf), representing the archers' guild; No. 7 Le Renard (Fox), the haberdashers' guild; No. 9 Le Cygne (Swan), the butchers' guild, where Karl Marx and Friedrich Engels wrote the *Communist Manifesto* in 1848; Nos. 24–25 La Chaloupe d'Or (Golden Galleon), the tailors' guild; and No. 26–27 Le Pigeon, representing the painters' guild, where novelist Victor Hugo stayed in 1852. Of particular interest are Nos. 29–33, the Maison du Roi, also called the Broodhuis in Flemish; it belonged not to a king but to the bakers' guild.

Manneken Pis

If it were not for the bus loads of tourists who gather in front of this little fellow to have their picture taken, it would be easy to walk past him—a strange mascot for a city.

Cheeky cherub Manneken Pis, meaning "pissing little boy," is one of Brussels' more amusing symbols. The bronze statuette, less than 60cm (2 feet) high, was created by Jérôme Duquesnoy the Elder in 1619. Known then as "Petit Julien," it has since become a legend. One story claims that the Julien on whom the statue was modelled was son of Duke Gottfried of Lorraine; another alleges that the statue urinated on a bomb fuse to save the Town Hall from destruction.

Often vandalized The statue was kidnapped by the English in 1745, as a way of getting at the people of Brussels; two years later the French took him away. In 1817 he was stolen by a French convict and was in pieces when he was recovered. The fragments were used to make the mould for the present statue. Even now he remains a temptation: He has been removed several times by drunk or angry students.

An extravagant wardrobe The French king Louis XV gave him a richly embroidered robe and the cross of Louis XIV as reparation for the bad behaviour of his soldiers in 1747. Now, Manneken Pis has hundreds of costumes, which you can see in the Musée de la Ville de Bruxelles (► 53).

DID YOU KNOW?

- In 1985 feminists demanded a female version of Manneken Pis and commissioned Janneken Pis (✉ Impasse de la Fidelité, off the Rue des Bouchers)
- Every 13 September Manneken Pis wears the uniform of a sergeant in the Regiment of Welsh Guards to celebrate the liberation of Brussels in 1944

INFORMATION

- ✚ E7; locator map B3
- ✉ Corner of rue de l'Etuve and rue du Chènet
- 🚇 Gare Centrale/Centraal Station or Bourse/Beurs
- 🚋 Tram 23, 52, 55, 56, 81
- 💰 Free
- ↔ Grand' Place (► 30), Hôtel de Ville (► 29), Musée de la Costume et de la Dentelle (► 52), Musée de la Ville de Bruxelles (► 53)
- ❓ See sign at the statue for the dates when it is dressed up

Top and left: *two of Manneken Pis' luxurious costumes*

31

Parc du Cinquantenaire

Built to celebrate 50 years of Belgian independence, the park has all you would imagine in the way of grand buildings—even its own Arc de Triomphe. It also has some surprises.

Top: *Autoworld*. Above: *the Arc de Triomphe*

INFORMATION

➕ H7–H8; locator map B2
✉ Main entrances rue de la Lo & avenue de Tervuren
🚇 Mérode, Schuman
🚌 20, 28, 36, 61, 67, 80; tram 81, 82
Autoworld
☎ 02 736 4165
🕐 10–6 (till 5 Oct–Mar)
🍴 Café
♿ Good 💶 Moderate
Army & Military History Museum
☎ 02 737 7811; www.klm-mra.be
🕐 Tue–Sun 9–12, 1–5
🍴 Café
♿ Poor 💶 Free
Museum of Art & History
☎ 02 741 7211; www.kmkg-mrah.be
🕐 Tue–Fri 9.30–5; Sat, Sun 10–5. Treasure Room 10–12, 1–4
🍴 Café
♿ Good 💶 Moderate

The most famous city park In 1880, Leopold II ordered the building of the Palais du Cinquantenaire, with two huge halls, to hold the National Exhibition in the park. For the next 25 years, the king dreamed about erecting an Arc de Triomphe. It was finally built in 1905 by Charles Girault, architect of the Petit Palais in Paris, with two colonnades added in 1918.

Remarkable monuments Several features here recall important international fairs. An Arab-inspired building, which housed a painted panorama of Cairo in an 1897 fair, is now Brussels' Grand Mosque. A small pavilion, known as Horta's pavilion (1889), was erected on designs by the architect to house the *haut-relief* of the *Human Passions*, by the sculptor Jef Lambeaux; it is now closed but you can peep in the window.

Grand but dusty museums One of the National Exhibition halls now showcases Autoworld, a prestigious collection of vintage cars from 1886 to the 1970s. The Musée Royal de l'Armée et d'Histoire Militaire incorporates an aviation museum with planes displayed in a huge hangar, and houses armour and weapons from medieval times to the present. The rich Musée Royal d'Art et d'Histoire, in the south wing of the Palais du Cinquantenaire, has artefacts from ancient civilizations, Belgian archaeological discoveries, and important European decorative arts and lace. Particularly worth seeing is the Treasure Room with medieval items, including reliquaries, textiles, and superb jewellery.

Musée d'Art Moderne

This museum puts modern Belgian artists in their context, and many of them shine, even among the great European stars. It also stages important temporary exhibitions.

20th-century Belgians Belgian artists are often overlooked in favour of their European and American contemporaries, so it is tempting to see something symbolic about the architecture of the Modern Art Museum, whose collection is buried in a multi-level subterranean building adjoining the Classical Art Museum. But by the time you have walked through the galleries of visual art, arranged chronologically (except for sculpture), you will certainly be seeing the light.

Fauvists and Surrealists Belgian artists, in the early 20th century, were particularly interested in fauvism and surrealism. Fauvism is best represented here by the works of Rik Wouters, Auguste Oleffe, and Léon Spilliaert. Surrealism followed, with its rejection of aesthetic values, growing out of post-World War I chaos. Belgians René Magritte and Paul Delvaux stand out as two stars of surrealism, and the museum collection includes one of Magritte's most famous paintings *The Dominion of Light*. Among the foreign artists represented here are Max Ernst, Francis Picabia, and Oskar Kokoshka.

Other movements The lower levels show Belgian futurism, abstract art, pop art, new realism, and minimal art. Particularly important here is the work of Marcel Broodthaers. A collection of works by Henri Matisse, Raoul Dufy, Picasso, Giorgio de Chirico, Marc Chagall, and Dali helps to put the Belgian artists in a wider context.

HIGHLIGHTS

- *L'Empire des Lumières* and others, René Magritte
- *The Flautist* and *The Woman with the Yellow Necklace*, Rik Wouters
- *In August, 1909*, Auguste Oleffe
- *The Public Voice* and *Pygmalion*, Paul Delvaux

INFORMATION

- F7; locator map B3–4
- 1–2 place Royale
- 02 508 3211; www.fine-arts-museum.be
- Tue–Sun 10–5
- Cafeteria
- Gare Centrale/Centraal Station or Trône/Troon
- 20, 34, 38, 54, 60, 71, 95, 96; tram 92, 93, 94
- Very good
- Moderate (free every 1st Wed of month from 1PM)
- Le Sablon (► 37), Musée d'Art Ancien (► 34), Musée des Instruments de Musique (► 35), place Royale (► 36)
- Regular temporary exhibitions as well as readings and music (information from Friends of the Museum ☎ 02 511 4116)

Top: Irène Hamoir, *René Magritte 1936*

Musée d'Art Ancien

HIGHLIGHTS

- *Landscape with the Fall of Icarus* and *The Census at Bethlehem*, Bruegel
- *The Ascent to Calvary* and *The Martyrdom of St. Lievin*, Rubens
- *Marat Murdered in his Bath*, Jacques-Louis David
- *La Justice d'Otton*, Dirk Bouts
- *The Scandalized Masks*, James Ensor
- *The Temptation of St. Antony*, School of Hieronymus Bosch

INFORMATION

- 🔳 F8; locator map B4
- ✉ 3 rue de la Régence
- ☎ 02 508 3211; www.fine-arts-museum.be
- 🕙 Tue–Sun 10–5
- 🍴 Cafeteria
- 🚉 Gare Centrale/ Centraal Station
- 🚌 20, 34, 38, 60, 71, 95, 96; tram 92, 93, 94
- ♿ Good
- 🎟 Moderate (free every 1st Wed of month from 1PM)
- 🔁 Le Sablon (➤ 37), Musée d'Art Moderne (➤ 33), place Royale (➤ 36), Musée des Instruments de Musique (➤ 35)
- ❓ Regular exhibitions, music, and readings (information from Friends of the Museum ☎ 02 511 4116)

This dull building houses a collection of art that is incredibly rich, created between the 15th and 19th centuries. The Bruegel and Rubens collections alone are worth travelling to see.

Museum history The Classical Art Museum and the neighbouring Modern Art Museum were founded by Napoleon Bonaparte in 1801 as the Museum of Brussels. The Classical Art Museum is housed in a building constructed in 1874–80 by Leopold II's colonial architect, Alphonse Balat. It underwent complete modernization in the 1980s and is now connected to the Museum of Modern Art by an underground passage.

Artistic riches The museum highlights how rich a period the 14th to 17th centuries were in Belgian art history, peaking with Hans Memling's marvellous canvases and the bizarre visions of Hieronymus Bosch. The museum's collection of the works of the Bruegels is world-class, second only to that in Vienna's Kunst-historisches Museum. Also shown are works by Rogier van der Weyden, Dirk Bouts, Hugo van der Goes, and, among later artists, Jacob Jordaens and van Dyck.

18th–19th centuries The museum's lower level contains 19th-century works by Gustave Courbet and Auguste Rodin. The central Forum, on the first floor, is home to a collection of 19th-century sculptures, including works by Jan van Kessels and Rodin, while the rooms off it contain masterpieces of the Romantic and Classical movements, including paintings by Delacroix.

Sculpture garden The sculpture collection in the garden beside the museum is less well known, but is excellent and well-arranged.

Musée des Instruments de Musique

The Museum of Musical Instruments is a pleasure to visit, both for its amazing collection and for the stunning art nouveau architecture of its "Old England" building.

The collection When in 1877 King Leopold II received a large number of Hindu instruments from Rajah Sourindo Mohun Tagore and at the same time the musicologist Jean-François Fetis donated his collection to the State, it was decided to create a Museum of Musical Instruments. Since then the museum has steadily acquired instruments from across the centuries and from all over the world. Today, with more than 7,000 instruments, one quarter of which are on display, it is one of the most important museums of its kind in the world. The bulk of the collection is European, from the Renaissance onwards. Every instrument is beautifully displayed, and some are astonishing pieces, like the glass harmonica designed by the American inventor and statesman Benjamin Franklin (1706–90), for which both Beethoven and Mozart wrote music, or the 18th century *pochettes*, tiny violins that violin teachers could carry in their pockets. Using a headset, visitors can listen to music played by the instrument at which they are looking. The museum has an extensive library, and a concert hall with breathtaking views over Brussels.

Old England Building The original museum, in the Sablon area, could no longer contain the collection, so it was decided in 2000 to move it to the empty four-floor building of the department store Old England. This was designed in 1899 by Paul Saintenoy who, inspired by the British Arts and Crafts movement, chose a grand art nouveau style with cast iron pillars, swirling wrought iron, and painted floral decoration.

DID YOU KNOW?

- Giacomo Puccini died in 1924 in a hospital near the place du Trône, in Brussels
- Adolphe Sax, who invented the saxophone in 1846, studied at the Royal Music Conservatoire in Brussels, where Clara Schumann, Hector Berlioz, Niccolo Paganini, Richard Wagner, and many others appeared

INFORMATION

- F7; locator map B4
- 2 rue Montagne de la Cour
- 02 545 0130; www.mim.fgov.be
- Tue, Wed, and Fri 9.30–5; Thu 9.30–8; Sat–Sun 10–5
- Bar and restaurant (££) on the top floor, with a summer terrace overlooking Brussels
- Gare Centrale/Centraal Station or Parc/Park
- Good
- Inexpensive
- Walking tours every Fri, 10.30–12, about the history of a particular instrument. Workshops in music, dance, and the making of instruments
- Musée d'Art Moderne (➤ 33), Musée d'Art Ancien (➤ 34), place Royale (➤ 36)

Place Royale

HIGHLIGHTS

- place du Musée
- Palace of Charles de Lorraine
- Fountain in parc de Bruxelles

INFORMATION

➕ F7–F8; locator map C4

🚇 Trône

🚌 20, 34, 38, 54, 60, 71, 95, 96; tram 92, 93, 94

Dynasty Museum

✉ 7 place des Palais

☎ 02 512 2821

🕐 Tue–Sun 10–6

♿ None 🎟 Free

Église de St.-Jacques-sur-Coudenberg

✉ place Royale

☎ 02 511 7836

🕐 Sat 10–6; Sun 10AM–11AM

♿ None 🎟 Free

Palais Royal

✉ place des Palais

☎ 02 551 2020

🕐 31 Jul–10 Sep: Tue–Sun 10.30–4.30

♿ Good 🎟 Free

Top: interior of the Palais du Roi. Right: Godefroid de Bouillon and the church of St.-Jacques-sur-Coudenberg

This elegant neoclassical square is anchored by some of Belgium's most powerful institutions: the Royal Palace, the Belgian Parliament, and the Law Courts.

Symmetrical square The place Royale, built between 1774–80, was originally an enclosed rectangle made up of eight palaces joined by porticoes. Among them is the Palace of Charles de Lorraine (1766), the lovely neoclassical building just off the square under which the Museum of Modern Art was built (➤ 33).

New Roads The addition of rue de la Régence on one side and rue Royale and the park on the other later made the square more accessible. In its centre stands the statue of Godefroid de Bouillon, who led the first crusade. The palaces now house public offices, the museums of Classical and Modern Art, and the interesting Dynasty Museum (chronicling the story of the Belgian royal family since 1830). On the east is the Église de St.-Jacques-sur-Coudenberg.

Palais Royal and parc de Bruxelles Nearby is place des Palais with Palais du Roi, the King's official residence, and parc de Bruxelles, the former monarch's hunting grounds. In the park, designed by Guimard (*c*1775), tree-lined avenues lead up to a central fountain. Horta's Palais des Beaux-Arts (1928) and the Film Museum are on rue Royale, while rue de la Loi has the Palais de la Nation, the Belgian Parliament.

Le Sablon

The Sablon district, with its Grand and Petit Sablon squares, is the centre of the antiques trade. It is also perfect for strolling, and its terraces are lovely places to sit and watch the world go by.

La place du Grand Sablon Many of Brussels' 17th-century aristocracy and bourgeoisie lived in this elegant square, which is now popular with antiques traders. The square has many specialist food shops, including Patisserie Wittamer (▶ 76), selling wonderful cakes, and Pierre Marcolini (▶ 77), with amazing chocolates.

La place du Petit Sablon Mayor Charles Buls commissioned this square in 1890. The statue of the Counts of Egmont and Horne, beheaded by the Duke of Alba because of their religion, was moved here from the Grand' Place and is surrounded by statues of 16th-century scholars and humanists. Behind the garden, the 16th-century Palais d'Egmont, rebuilt in the early 20th century after a fire, is used for receptions by the Ministry of Foreign Affairs.

Église de Notre Dame du Sablon The 15th-century church of Notre Dame du Sablon is a fine example of flamboyant Gothic architecture, built over an earlier chapel with a miraculous statue of the Virgin Mary. A hemp weaver from Antwerp heard celestial voices telling her to steal the Madonna statue at the church where she worshipped and take it to Brussels. The choir and stained-glass windows are particularly beautiful. Many statues, pinnacles, turrets, and parts of the facade were finished or restored in 19th-century neo-Gothic style.

HIGHLIGHTS

- Église de Notre Dame du Sablon
- Statues on the place du Petit Sablon
- Antiques market and shops
- Garden behind Palais d'Egmont
- Patisserie Wittamer

Top: *the antiques market*
Above: *chocolates*

INFORMATION

- E8–F8; locator map B4
- Church: 02 511 5741
- Church: Mon–Fri 9–5; Sat 10–5; Sun 1–5
- Restaurants, cafés
- 20, 48; tram 91, 92, 93, 94
- Good
- Les Marolles (▶ 38), art museums (▶ 33, 34), place Royale (▶ 36), Musée des Instruments de Musique (▶ 35)
- Antiques market Sat 9–6; Sun 9–2 (▶ 60); *Ommegang* procession (▶ 62)

Les Marolles

Dwarfed by the Palais de Justice and hemmed in by the elegant Sablon quarter, the Marolles is a reminder of working-class Brussels, with its narrow cobbled streets and junk shops.

DID YOU KNOW?

● Pieter Bruegel, born 1525, lived at 152 rue Haute

INFORMATION

✚ E8; locator map B4
✉ The area around place du Jeu de Balle
🍴 Restaurants nearby
🚇 Porte de Hal/Halleepoort
🚌 20, 48; tram 91
♿ Few
↔ Le Sablon (➤ 37), avenue Louise (➤ 39), Église Notre-Dame-de-la-Chapelle (➤ 55), Palais de Justice(➤ 56)
❓ Junk market daily 7AM–2PM

Top: *junk market in the place du Jeu de Balle*

The heart and soul of Brussels Developed in the 17th century as a residential area for craftsmen working on the palaces and grand houses of the Upper City, the Marolles remained a lively working-class area until the 1870s, when the River Senne was covered and many artisans moved farther out. In the 19th century, part of the Marolles was demolished to make way for the imposing Palais de Justice. In the shadow of this symbol of law and order, the district became a crumbling haven for the city's poor and for Maghrebi immigrants from northwest Africa.

Where to go The Marolles stretches roughly from the Porte de Hal to the Église Notre-Dame-de-la-Chapelle; rue Blaes and rue Haute are its main thoroughfares. The streets around the place du Jeu de Balle are full of snack bars, smoky traditional cafés, and junk shops. The junk market, held on the place du Jeu de Balle, is the place to look for unusual objects at bargain prices, especially on Sunday mornings, the market's liveliest time.

Property speculation The Marolles is changing quickly as property speculators, art galleries, and the fashionable crowd move in. Neither the indigenous inhabitants nor new immigrant families have the money to save their homes from the wrecker's ball, but action groups are working for the preservation of the Marolles and the restoration of its buildings.

Avenue Louise

Once a showpiece of Belgian progress, avenue Louise is now one of the places where you'll see ladies heading for the designer boutiques jostling with kids from the fast-food joints.

Imperial design It's not hard to detect the stamp of Leopold II on avenue Louise. The thoroughfare was laid out in 1864 and was named after his eldest daughter. Stretching for a mile, as wide as a Parisian boulevard and just about pencil-straight (except where it swerves to avoid the Abbaye de la Cambre, ➤ 54), it remains the link between central Brussels and the Bois de la Cambre, with its attractive park and lake, and the countryside beyond.

Shopping This is where Brussels bureaucrats come to spend their money; they crowd the many smart cafés, spilling onto the streets, and part with hundreds of euros in its stores. It is one of Brussels' main shopping streets, and is lined with boutiques, interior designers, showrooms, art galleries, hotels, and restaurants. Near place Louise, not far from Leopold's Palais de Justice, café-lined alleys run off the avenue. Beyond place Stéphanie (named after another of Leopold II's daughters), the avenue widens, the buildings get higher, the traffic increases, and shop prices climb. Head for the galleries, the most famous of which are the Galeries de la Toison d'Or (Golden Fleece Galleries) and Galerie Louise on the intersecting avenue de la Toison d'Or.

Horta here At 224 avenue Louise, Victor Horta designed the Hôtel Solvay (1894–98), along with its furniture and silverware. Look through the glass door to glimpse the interior. Rue du Bailli, off the avenue, leads to rue Américaine and the Musée de Victor Horta (➤ 40).

HIGHLIGHTS

- Hôtel Solvay
- Chanel and other boutiques
- Galeries de la Toison d'Or
- Abbaye de la Cambre

INFORMATION

- E8, F9–F10, G10; locator map B4
- avenue Louise
- Restaurants nearby
- Louise/Louiza
- 34, 54, 60; tram 91, 92, 93, 94
- Good
- Les Marolles (➤ 38), Le Sablon (➤ 37), Palais de Justice (➤ 56)

Top: *window-shopping in the avenue Louise*

Musée de Victor Horta

Many of the grand buildings designed by art nouveau architect Victor Horta have been destroyed, but here in his house in the rue Américaine, the flowing lines and the play of light and space clarify his vision.

New Style Victor Horta (1861–1947) built these two houses on the rue Américaine as his home and studio between 1898 and 1901. Now a museum, they illustrate the break he made from traditional town houses, with their large, sombre rooms. Horta's are spacious and airy, full of mirrors, white tiles, and stained-glass windows. A light shaft in the middle of the house illuminates a banister so gracious and flowing that you just want to slide down it. The attention to detail in the house is amazing, even down to the last door handle, all designed in fluid art nouveau style.

Art nouveau in St.-Gilles Although Horta's is the only house open to the public, there are other interesting properties in wealthy St.-Gilles. Strolling around the area between the rue Defacqz and the prison of St.-Gilles you can admire several examples of art nouveau style, dating from the late 19th to early 20th centuries. Paul Hankar designed the Ciambarlani and Janssens mansions at Nos. 48 and 50 rue Defacqz, and his own house at No. 71. One of the most beautiful art nouveau facades in Brussels, designed by Albert Roosenboom, is 85 rue Faider. At No. 83 rue de Livourne you can see the private house of the architect Octave Van Rysselberghe, who also built the Otlet mansion at No. 48 rue de Livourne. The Hannon mansion, built at No. 1 avenue de la Jonction by Jules Brunfaut, is now a photographer's gallery; look for the impressive fresco by Paul-Albert Baudouin in the staircase.

DID YOU KNOW?

- Art nouveau originated in Britain in the 1880s but Brussels architects Paul Hankar, Henri van de Velde, and especially Victor Horta made it completely their own style
- ARAU trips visit other art nouveau houses (▶ 20)
- The brochure "Le guide des décors céramiques à Bruxelles de 1880 à 1940" by Chantal Declève takes in 10 walks along the most beautiful art nouveau facades in Brussels and is available from the tourist office on the Grand' Place, the Musée de Victor Horta, and good bookshops

INFORMATION

- ✚ E10; locator map B2
- ✉ 25 rue Américaine
- ☎ 02 543 0490
- 🕐 Tue–Sun 2–5.30
- 🍴 Horta
- 🚌 54, 60; tram 81, 82, 91, 92
- ♿ Few
- 💰 Moderate

Top: the art nouveau staircase in the Musée de Victor Horta

De Vesten en Poorten

To understand Bruges' layout, take a ride or walk around its walls, especially on the east side, where the gates, ramparts, windmills, and canals give the impression of containing the city, as they have done for 600 years.

Fortified Bruges Bruges' original fortifications (de Vesten en Poorten) date back to AD 1000, but nothing survives of the six original bastion gates beyond an inscription on Blinde Ezelstraat marking the location of the south gate. Between 1297 and 1300, as the medieval city grew increasingly wealthy, new defenses were built; of the seven new gates, four survive, two in the east—Kruispoort (Cross Gate, 1402), with a drawbridge, and Gentpoort (Ghent Gate, 14th century) with twin towers—and two in the west—Bruges' only two-way gate, Smedenpoort (Blacksmiths' Gate, 14th century), and Ezelpoort (Donkeys' Gate, rebuilt in the 17th and 18th centuries).

Blowing in the wind The ramparts that linked the gates on the east side were used as raised platforms for windmills. Of the 25 mills marked on a panorama of Bruges from 1562, only four stand along the canal between Kruispoort and Dampoort today, and all are of more recent date. The first mill when viewed coming from Kruispoort, Bonne Chiere (Good Show), was built in 1888 and reconstructed in 1911, but has never worked. The second mill, Sint-Janshuysmolen (St. John's House Mill), near the intersection of Kruisvest and Rolweg, was built by bakers in 1770 (➤ 57). The third mill, De Nieuwe Papegaai (New Parrot), a 1790 oil mill, was moved to Bruges from Beveren in 1970. A fourth mill, constructed in the mid-1990s, is near the Dampoort.

DID YOU KNOW?

- The statue of St. Adrian (1448, remodelled 1956) on Gentpoort was carved by Jan van Cutsegem to ward off plague.
- Smedenpoort's bronze skull (hung there in 1911) replaces the real skull of a traitor.
- Of the 25 windmills in Bruges in 1562, 23 still existed in the 19th century, but between 1863 and 1879, 20 of them were pulled down.
- The 6.5km- (4-mile-) long ramparts of Bruges were laid out as parks in the 19th century and are pleasant for walking

Top: *contained by canals*
Below: *the Gentpoort*

Kathedraal St.-Salvator

HIGHLIGHTS

- *Martyr's Death of St. Hippolytus*, Dirk Bouts' triptych (1470–75)
- *Last Supper*, Pieter Pourbus
- 14th-century *Tanner's Panel*
- *The Mother of Sorrows*
- Baroque statue of God the Father
- Eekhoute Cross in shoemakers' chapel
- Eight tapestries by Jaspar van der Borght

INFORMATION

- ➕ bIII; locator map E3
- ✉ Zuidzandstraat
- 🕐 Mon 2–5.45; Tue–Fri 8.30–11.45, 2–5.45; Sat 8.30–11.45, 2–3.30; Sun 9–10.15, 3–5.45. Museum open afternoons only
- 🚌 1, 2, 3, 4, 5, 8, 9, 11, 13, 16
- ♿ Very good
- 💰 Cathedral free; museum inexpensive
- 🔁 Onze-Lieve-Vrouwekerk (➤ 45), Gruuthuse Museum (➤ 46), Markt (➤ 48)
- 🎵 Important concerts and church services during public hols, check with tourist office

Top: *one of the Brussels tapestries in the cathedral*

The Kathedraal St.-Salvator, together with the belfry and the Onze-Lieve-Vrouwekerk, towers above Bruges. The artworks inside are a reminder of the cathedral's long and eventful history.

The cathedral A house of prayer existed in this location as early as the 9th century; it was dedicated to St. Saviour and to St. Eloi, who is believed to have founded an earlier wooden church here in 660. The present cathedral was built towards the end of the 13th century. This cathedral was damaged by fires on several occasions, and in 1798 many of its treasures were stolen by the French, who put the building and its contents up for auction the following year. However, wealthy Brugeans bought a lot back. The neo-Romanesque top was added to the remarkable tower in 1844–46 and the spire in 1871. The oldest sections of the tower of the present church date back to 1127.

Sculptures and tapestries The cathedral houses some splendid sculptures and wonderful church furniture. The large statue of God the Father (1682) by Arthur Quellinus is one of the best baroque sculptures in Bruges. The doors of the shoemakers' chapel, as well as the sculptures in the Cross chapel and the Peter and Paul chapel, are superb examples of late Gothic oak carving. Six of the eight 18th-century tapestries in the choir and transept, illustrating the life of Christ, were woven in Brussels.

Flemish art in the museum The museum displays most of the church's collection. There are several wonderful pieces of 15th-century Flemish art among the 120 or so paintings, and there are gold and silver artefacts, pottery, and manuscripts.

Begijnhof

Many Flemish cities have kept their *begijnhof*, but the one in Bruges is undoubtedly one of the oldest and most picturesque, a place of exquisite silence and repose.

Our Lady of Good Will

Closed court Beginning in the 12th century pious women started to live in communities, spending their days praying, making lace, looking after the sick and old, and sometimes taking monastic vows. They lived apart from the city in a *begijnhof* (*béguinage*) or closed court, whose entrance was shut at night. The Bruges *begijnhof* consists of a number of houses arranged around one such square. Since 1927 it has been occupied by Benedictine nuns, whose severe black-and-white habits are a reminder of those of the *béguines* who once lived there. Several times a day the nuns walk to the church through the green garden at the side of the square. The square is particularly beautiful in early spring, when it is abloom with daffodils.

The church The simple church (1605) is dedicated to St. Elisabeth of Hungary, whose portrait hangs above the entrance. She also appears in a painting by Bruges master Lodewijk de Deyster (1656–1711). The most important work is the statue of Our Lady of Spermalie (*c*1240), the oldest statue of the Virgin in Bruges. On the left wall as you face the altar is a superb statue of Our Lady of Good Will. The remarkable alabaster sculpture of the Lamentation of Christ at the High Altar dates from the early 17th century.

A *béguine's* house The tiny museum at the back of the church, a reconstruction of a 17th-century *béguine's* house, complete with furniture and household goods, gives an idea of how the community used to live.

HIGHLIGHTS

- The square
- Statue of Our Lady of Spermalie
- *Béguine's* house

INFORMATION

- ✠ bIV; locator map E4
- ✉ Wijngaardplein
- ☎ 050 33 00 11
- 🕐 Church and *begijnhof* summer: daily 9–7. Winter: daily 9–6. Museum daily 10–12, 1.45–5
- 🚊 1, 2
- ♿ Good
- 🎟 Free. Museum inexpensive
- ↔ Memling Museum (► 44)

43

St.-Janshospitaal en Memling Museum

DID YOU KNOW?

- On the back of *The Mystical Marriage of St. Catherine*, Memling painted the donors
- Jan Florein donated *The Adoration of the Magi*, and is shown kneeling on the left of the painting
- Adriaan Reins, friar of the hospital, is on the side panel of *The Lamentation of Christ*
- Maria Portal

INFORMATION

- ➕ bIV; locator map E3
- ✉ Mariastraat 38
- ☎ 050 44 87 43
- 🕐 Daily 9.30–5 (closed on Wed Oct–Mar)
- 🚻 1
- 🍴 Restaurants nearby
- ♿ Very good
- 💵 Expensive
- 🔄 Canals (➤ 61)

Madonna with apple, *Memling 1487*

Among the must-sees of Bruges are the Hans Memling works on show here, 15th-century landmarks in the history of art. It's a bonus that the building that houses them is also a gem.

The hospital St. John's, founded in the 12th century, is one of Europe's oldest hospices (medieval hospitals) and continued functioning until 1976, when medical care was moved to a new building. The Gothic Maria Portal (*c*1270) on Mariastraat is the original gate. Subsequent buildings include a tower, central ward, brewery, monastery, bathhouse, cemetery (all 14th century), St. Cornelius Chapel (15th century), and a convent for the hospital's sisters (1539). The 17th-century dispensary, with exhibits of ancient remedies, and the church are particularly interesting. The wards were renovated in 2001 and some were converted into cafés and shops.

The Memling masterpieces As St. John's reputation as a hospital grew, so did its wealth. Its funds were invested, with inspiration, in the works of Hans Memling, a German painter who had settled in Bruges by 1465 and died one of its richest citizens in 1494. Four of the six works on display here were commissioned by St. John's friars and sisters, the most famous being the *Ursula Shrine* (1489), a relic box in the shape of a church, gilded and painted with scenes from the life of St. Ursula. The triptych *Mystical Marriage of St. Catherine* (1479) was commissioned for the chapel's main altar, as were two smaller triptychs—*The Adoration of the Magi* (1479) and *The Lamentation of Christ* (1480). The diptych *Madonna with Child* (1487) and the portrait of *The Sibylla Sambetha* (1480) were moved here from the former St. Julian's hospice in 1815.

Onze-Lieve-Vrouwekerk

Beneath the monumental brick tower in the Church of our Lady, the religious feeling is palpable, heightened by the aroma of incense, the magnificent sculptures, and the stunning paintings all around you.

One of Bruges' seven wonders Although there was a chapel here about 1,000 years ago, the choir and facade on Mariastraat date from the 13th century, and the aisles and superbly restored Paradise Porch from the 14th and 15th centuries. The church's most striking feature is the tower, 122m (400-foot) high, begun in the 13th century.

Artworks The star attraction is the *Madonna and Child* by Michelangelo (1475–1564). Other sculptures include a rococo pulpit (1743) by the Bruges painter Jan Garemijn, some fine altars, and the Lanchals monument in the Lanchals chapel (both 15th century). The prayer balcony connected to the Gruuthuse mansion (▶ 46) enabled the lords of the Gruuthuse to attend services directly from home. The church contains some important 16th-century Flemish paintings, including works by Gerard David, Pieter Pourbus, and Adriaan Isenbrandt. The valuable *Katte of Beversluys*, kept in the sacristy, weighs 3kg (7 pounds) and is embellished with enamel and precious stones.

Mausoleums Both Charles the Bold, who died in 1477, and Mary of Burgundy, who died in 1482 after a hunting fall, are buried here in superb adjacent mausoleums moved to the Lanchals chapel in 1806 and returned here in 1979. Excavations revealed beautiful 16th-century frescoes in other tombs and also the fact that Mary's remains were buried with the heart of her son Philip the Fair.

HIGHLIGHTS

- Brick tower
- Paradise Porch
- Mausoleums of Charles the Bold and Mary of Burgundy
- *Madonna and Child*, Michaelangelo
- *The Adoration of the Shepherds*, Pieter Poubus
- *Our Lady of the Seven Sorrows*, probably by Adriaan Isenbrandt
- *The Transfiguration of Mount Tabor*, Gerard David

INFORMATION

- ✚ blV; locator map E3
- ✉ Mariastraat
- 🕐 Church: Mon–Sat 10–11.30, 2.30–5; Sun 2.30–5 (4.30 in winter). Mausoleums: Sat 10–11.30, 2.30–4.30 (4 in winter)
- 🚋 1
- ♿ Very good
- 💰 Church free; mausoleums inexpensive
- 🔁 St.-Salvator's Kathedraal (▶ 42), Begijnhof (▶ 43), Memling Museum (▶ 44), Gruuthuse Museum (▶ 46), Groeninge Museum (▶ 47)
- ❓ Weekend services: Sat 5 and 6.30PM; Sun 11AM

Mausoleum of Charles the Bold

45

Gruuthuse Museum

INFORMATION

The peaceful facade and courtyard of the Gruuthuse Palace transport you back to medieval times. And it is a delight to stroll around the adjacent Arentspark and watch boats pass under the Boniface Bridge, one of Bruges' most romantic corners.

The palace of Gruuthuse Built in the late 15th century by humanist and arts lover Louis van Gruuthuse, this now houses the Gruuthuse Museum, a fascinating collection of antiques and applied arts, well laid out in a series of 22 numbered rooms. There are some fine sculptures, including an early 16th-century Gothic kneeling angel rendered in oak; the impressive *Christ, Man of Sorrows* (c1500), and the 15th century *Reading Madonna* by Adriaan van Wezel.

Bruggean Tapestries Well-preserved 17th-century examples in the Tapestry Room represent the Seven Liberal Arts; and some fine baroque wool and silk counterparts in Room 8 have pastoral themes, including the very excellent comic-strip like tapestry the *Country Meal*. Rooms 18 and 19 hold a precious lace collection. Room 16 is the prayer room, in the form of a balcony, that looks down into the Onze-Lieve-Vrouwekerk (► 45). Together with the kitchen, it is the oldest part of the building.

Brangwyn Museum (Arents Huis) Next door is the Arents Huis, which houses four collections donated by wealthy Belgians to Bruges: pewter from the 18th to the 20th centuries; 18th- and 19th-century works of art, including exquisite china; a collection of mother-of-pearl; and the world's largest collection of paintings by Frank Brangwyn (1867–1956), a Bruges-born British painter who studied under William Morris.

Top: a delicate ironwork sign outside refers to the brewhouse origins of the palace

Groeninge Museum

Jan van Eyck's serene *Portrait of Margaretha van Eyck* and Gerard David's gruesome *The Judgement of Cambyses*, portraying a magistrate being skinned alive, are so arresting that it is easy to overlook the contemporary art here.

The Flemish Primitives   The 15th-century Flemish Primitives were so named in the 19th century to express a desire to recapture the pre-Renaissance simplicity in art. Room 1 shows works by van Eyck (*c*1390–1441), including the *Madonna with Canon Joris van der Paele* and the *Portrait of Margaretha van Eyck*, the painter's wife. Two works by Hans Memling—the *Moreel Triptych* and two panels of *The Annunciation*—are also present. Also displayed here are works by Rogier van der Weyden, Hugo van der Goes, and the last of the Flemish Primitives, Gerard David, including his *The Judgement of Cambyses* and the large triptych *The Baptism of Christ*. In Room 7 the 16th-century works of Pieter Pourbus illustrate the Italian influence on Flemish style. In Room 8, look for the lovely baroque *Portrait of a Brugean Family* by Jacob van Oost (1601–71).

Modern Flemish masters   Emile Claus (1849–1924) and Rik Wouters (1882–1916) are well represented. Also look for James Ensor's *Le Parc aux Oiselles* and works of Gust de Smet, Gustave van de Woestijne, and Rik Slabbinck; works by Constant Permeke represent the best of Flemish expressionism. There are two paintings by Paul Delvaux and one by René Magritte. The last room shows works from the 1950s to the 1970s by Brugeans Luc Peire and Gilbert Swimberghe, and Roger Raveel; it also contains a cabinet by avant-garde artist Marcel Broodthaers (1924–75).

HIGHLIGHTS

- *Portrait of Margaretha van Eyck*, van Eyck
- *Moreel Triptych* and *Annunciation*, Hans Memling
- *Portrait of a Brugean Family*, Jacob van Oost
- *The Assault*, René Magritte

INFORMATION

- ✚ clll; locator map E3
- ✉ Dijver 12
- ☎ 050 44 87 43
- 🕐 Daily 9.30–5 (closed Tue in winter)
- 🍴 Cafeteria
- ▣ 1
- ♿ Good
- 💰 Expensive
- ⟷ Markt (➤ 48), canals (➤ 61)

Top: Portrait of a Brugean Family. Below: *the* Moreel Triptych

Markt

DID YOU KNOW?

- During the Brugse Metten massacre (18 May 1302), Flemish workers and citizens killed hundreds of occupying French soldiers
- The statue of Jan Breydel and Pieter de Coninck was unveiled three times
- The Belfry tower is 83m (272 feet) high, has 366 steps to the top, and leans southeast
- The tower has a four-octave carillon of 47 bells cast by Joris Dumery in 1748
- Combined weight of bells is 27 tons
- The carillon marks the quarter hour

INFORMATION

- ![] bIII; locator map E3
- ✉ Markt
- ◷ Belfry daily 9.30–5
- 🍴 Several restaurants and tea rooms nearby
- ▣ 1, 2, 3, 4, 5, 6, 7, 8, 9, 11, 13, 15, 16, 17, 25
- ♿ Good
- 🏛 Belfry tower moderate
- ↔ Kathedraal St.-Salvator (► 42), Burg (► 49), Basilica of the Holy Blood (► 50)
- ❓ Carillon concerts Oct–June 14: Wed, Sat, Sun 2.15–3. Jun 15–Sep: Mon, Wed, Sat 9–10PM; Sun 2.15–3

The Belfry, emblematic of Bruges' medieval power and freedom, dominates the city's main square, the Markt (Market). The square is ringed with Gothic and neo-Gothic buildings.

The city's core This square has always been at the heart of Bruges with its historic and attractive buildings. A weekly market was held here from 1200 onwards until it was moved to t'Zand in 1983. The late 19th-century neo-Gothic Provincial Government Palace and the Central Post Office (1887–1921) stand on the site of the former Waterhalles, a huge covered dock where ships moored. Across Sint-Amandstraat is Craenenburgh House, where Maximilian of Austria was locked up in 1488. The square's north side was once lined with tilers' and fishmongers' guildhalls, which are now restaurants.

Heroes There is a bronze statue (1887) of two medieval Brugean heroes, Jan Breydel and Pieter de Coninck, who in 1302 led the Brugse Metten, the massacre of hundreds of occupying French soldiers by Flemish workers. The same year saw the rebellion of the Flemish against the French king, Philip IV, at the Battle of the Golden Spurs, resulting in Flanders' independence.

The Halles and Belfry The origins of the Halles (town hall and treasury) and the Belfry (called "Halletoren" in Bruges) go back to the 13th century, when the Halles were originally the seat of the municipality and the city's treasury. From the balcony, the bailiff read the "Halles commands," while the bells warned citizens of approaching danger or enemies.

Burg

This historic enclave evokes medieval Bruges better than any other part of the city. Its impressive buildings once contained the offices of the church, city, county, and judicial authorities.

A separate entity Until the 18th century, the Burg was walled in and locked with four gates. The north side of the square was dominated by the 10th-century St. Donatian's Church, sold by auction and torn down soon after in 1799. (Under the trees, there is a scale model of the church, and some of its foundations can be seen in the basement of the Holiday Inn hotel.)

The square The whole of the square's west side was once the Steen, an impressive 11th-century tower; only the porch beside the stairs to the Basilica of the Holy Blood (▶ 50) remains. On the southeast side of the square, to the left of the Town Hall and across Blinde Ezelstraat, is the Flemish-Renaissance Civil Recorders' House (1535–37). On the eastern side of the square is the Palace of the Brugse Vrije (1722–27), a rural region along the coast that was subordinate to Bruges. The building, home to the Palace of Justice until the 1980s, now houses the tourist office and a museum containing the *Mantelpiece of Charles V*, a Renaissance work of art by Lancelot Blondeel.

The Town Hall Built between 1376 and 1420, Bruges' Town Hall is the oldest and one of the most beautiful in Belgium. Although its turreted sandstone facade dates from 1376, the statues on its Gothic facade date from the 1970s. The Gothic Room, with its superb ceiling, is where Philip the Good called together the first States General of the Ancient Low Countries in 1464; it is now reserved for private functions.

Above: *detail of the Town Hall facade*

HIGHLIGHTS

- Gothic Room in the Town Hall
- Town Hall facade
- Mantelpiece of Charles V in Brugse Vrije museum

INFORMATION

- ✛ bIII; locator map E3
- ✉ Burg
- ☎ Tourist office: 050 44 86 86
- ◉ Town Hall (Gothic Room): daily 9.30–5. Museum: Brugse Vrije daily 9.30–12.30, 1.30–5 (closed Tue in winter)
- 🍽 Restaurants nearby
- 🚌 All buses to the Markt
- ♿ Very good
- 💷 Inexpensive
- ↔ Markt (▶ 48), Basilica of the Holy Blood (▶ 50)
- ❓ Concerts in summer

49

Heilig Bloedbasiliek

INFORMATION

➕ blll; locator map E3

✉ Burg 10

🕐 Apr–Sep: daily 9.30–12, 2–6. Oct–Mar: Thu–Tue 10–12, 2–4. Closed some hols and during services

🚌 All buses to the Markt

♿ None

💵 Inexpensive

❓ Sun services 8AM–11AM. Worship of the Holy Blood Fri 8.30–11.45, 3–4. Ascension Day 8.30–10.15 and from 6PM

Top: *Heilig Bloedkapel facade*. Below: *Heilig Bloed Procession, May*

The Romanesque Chapel of the Holy Blood, shrouded in mystery, is rich with the atmosphere of the Middle Ages. Even travellers who are casual about religion tend to fall silent in the face of the intense devotion of the worshippers here.

Holy Blood Thierry of Alsace, Count of Flanders and a crusader, is said to have received the relic with the blood of Jesus from the Patriarch of Jerusalem. He brought it to Bruges in 1150. Stored in two crystal vials, the relic is exhibited every Friday for adoration on the Blessing Altar in the Chapel of the Holy Blood, or the upper church. This area was originally Romanesque, but has been heavily restored in clumsy Gothic style. The original 15th-century stained-glass windows are now in London's Victoria & Albert Museum; those here are 19th-century copies.

Silver and Gold The museum contains paintings, tapestries, silver, and the Reliquary of the Holy Blood. This gold and silver reliquary (1617) was made by Renaissance goldsmith Jan Crabbe and is decorated with pearls and precious stones. Each year it is carried around the city during the Procession of the Holy Blood (▶ 62).

St. Basil's Chapel The lower chapel, a small Romanesque three-aisled church supported on thick sandstone columns, was built around 1139 on designs by Count Thierry of Alsace. It is dedicated to the Virgin Mary and to St. Basil, the patron saint of bricklayers. The wooden *Virgin with Child* (c1300) is one of Bruges' most beautiful Gothic statues. The less refined 19th-century *Ecce Homo* in the side chapel is much adored. Bruges' oldest sculpture, a low-relief baptism (c1100), stands in the side-chapel passage.

BRUSSELS' & BRUGES'
best

Museums

RENÉ MAGRITTE

The house where the surrealist painter René Magritte and his wife lived until the mid-1950s has been restored and now contains a modest collection of his works—more can be seen at the Musée d'Art Moderne (➤ 33). The house is surprisingly plain but fans of Magritte will recognise details and views familiar from his paintings.

✉ 135 rue Esseghem, Brussels ☎ 02 428 2626
⏰ Wed–Sun 10–6
🚇 Pannenhuis

MUSÉE DE COSTUME ET DE LA DENTELLE

Here you will find a fine collection of old lace, embroidery, and costumes; courses in lace-making; and interesting temporary exhibitions.

➕ E7 ✉ 6 rue de la Violette ☎ 02 512 7709 ⏰ Mon, Tue, Thu, Fri 10–12.30, 1.30–5; Sat, Sun 2–4.30 🚇 Gare Centrale/Centraal Station or Bourse/Beurs 🚌 29, 34, 38, 47, 48, 60, 63, 65, 66, 71, 95, 96; tram 23, 52, 55, 56, 81 ♿ Good 💰 Moderate

MUSÉE DAVID ET ALICE VAN BUUREN

This delightful museum is in the van Buuren's elegant private house, built and furnished in the art deco style. The interior and the gardens are stunning, but the art collection of the banker and his wife is equally remarkable, including Bruegel and Van Gogh.

➕ E11 ✉ 41 avenue Léo Errera ☎ 02 343 4851 ⏰ Sun 1–5.30; Mon 2–5.30 🚌 60; tram 23, 90 ♿ Few wheelchair facilities 💰 Moderate

MUSÉE ROYAL DE L'AFRIQUE CENTRALE

When it opened in 1897, the Royal Museum for Central Africa glorified the Belgian presence in Africa. Now, despite its grand facade, it is a musty place, popular with children for its dioramas with stuffed animals and for its large collection of creepy crawlies.

Below: *Musée Royal de L'Afrique Centrale (Royal Museum for Central Africa)*

The grounds are worth a visit—attractively laid out formal gardens, flanked by lakes and pleasant woods.

➕ Off map 🖂 13 Leuvensesteenweg, Tervuren ☎ 02 769 5211; www.africamuseum.be 🕐 Tue–Fri 10–5; weekends 10–6 🍴 Cafeteria 🚊 Tram 44 from metro station Montgomery ♿ Good 💷 Moderate

MUSÉE DE LA VILLE DE BRUXELLES

This 19th-century building, a careful reconstruction of the original Maison du Roi, is devoted to the city's history in all aspects, and displays a fine collection of paintings, tapestries, maps, and manuscripts, as well as the extensive wardrobe of Manneken Pis (➤ 31).

➕ E7 🖂 Maison du Roi, Grand' Place ☎ 02 279 4350 🕐 Apr–Sep: Tue–Fri 10–5; Sat–Sun 10–1. Oct–Mar: Tue–Fri 10–4, Sat–Sun 10–1 🚇 Bourse/Beurs, Gare Centrale/Centraal Station 🚊 29, 34, 47, 48, 60, 63, 65, 66, 71, 95, 96; tram 23, 52, 55, 56, 81 ♿ Few 💷 Moderate

BRUGES

In the Top 25
22 **GROENINGE MUSEUM** (➤ 47)
21 **GRUUTHUSE MUSEUM** (➤ 46)
19 **MEMLING MUSEUM** (➤ 44)

MUSEUM ONZE-LIEVE-VROUW TER POTTERIE

A wonderful little museum in a former hospital (13th–17th centuries) that has been run as a nursing-home since the 15th century. There are sculptures, 15th and 16th-century paintings, tapestries, and furniture. The church has one of Bruges' finest baroque interiors.

➕ cll 🖂 Potterierei 79 ☎ 050 44 87 77 🕐 Apr–Sep: daily 9.30–12.30, 1.30–5. Oct–Mar: Thu–Tue 9.30–12.30, 1.30–5 🚊 4 ♿ Very good 💷 Moderate

MUSEUM VOOR VOLKSKUNDE

Bruges' past is recalled in these 17th-century almshouses. Period rooms and exhibits explain the traditional professions, popular worship, and costumes.

➕ clll 🖂 Rolweg 40 ☎ 050 44 87 64 🕐 Daily 9.30–5 🍴 Medieval inn In de Zwarte Kat 🚊 4, 6 ♿ Good 💷 Moderate

Above left: *Ter Potterie Museum*
Below: *Museum voor Volkskunde*

53

Churches

THE BRUSSELS *BÉGUINAGE*

The church of St. John the Baptist, the finest example of Flemish baroque in the country, and the rue du Béguinage are all that are left of the once flourishing *Béguinage* founded in the 13th century outside the city walls. The former gardens were used to build the Hospice Pachéco, created in 1824 and still in use today.

➕ E6 ✉ place du Béguinage ☎ 02 521 1383 ⏰ Thu–Mon 10–12, 2–5 🚌 58, 61; tram 92, 93, 94 ♿ Good 🎫 Inexpensive

Above: *Abbaye de la Cambre*
Below: *Notre Dame de la Chapelle, detail*

BRUSSELS

In the Top 25

3 CATHÉDRALE ST.-MICHEL ET STE.-GUDULE (➤ 28)
12 ÉGLISE DE NOTRE DAME DU SABLON (➤ 37)
11 ÉGLISE ST.-JACQUES-SUR-COUDENBERG (➤ 36)

ABBAYE DE LA CAMBRE

Founded in 1201 for the Cistercian Order, the abbey was extensively rebuilt during the 16th and 18th centuries. Now it houses the National Geographical Institution. There is also a 14th-century church.

➕ G10 ✉ avenue E. Duray ☎ 02 648 1121 ⏰ Mon–Fri 9–12, 3–6; Sat 8–12.30, 3–6; Sun 9–12.30 🚌 Tram 23, 90, 93, 94 ♿ Few 🎫 Free

BASILIQUE DE KOEKELBERG

The basilica's massive green dome is one of Brussels' landmarks, but the interior is cold and gloomy. Built between 1905 and 1979 as the world's largest art deco church, it was meant to be a symbol of unification between Belgium's Flemish and French-speaking communities. The views from the dome are superb.

➕ C5 ✉ 1 parvis de la Basilique ☎ 02 425 8822 ⏰ Daily 8–6 (until 5 in winter). Dome Mar-Oct: Mon–Fri 11 and 3 🚌 Simonis, then tram 19 🎫 Free; entry to the dome inexpensive

COLLÉGIALE DES STS.-PIERRE ET GUIDON

The Romanesque crypt is 11th century, but the superb
Gothic church with frescoes is from the 14th to 16th
centuries. The altar is illuminated by light filtering
through the lovely stained glass above. The rare Celtic
tombstone is believed to mark the grave of St. Guidon.
🚹 B8 ⊠ place de la Vaillance ☎ 02 521 7438 🕐 Mon, Tue,
Thu–Sat 9–12, 2–6; Wed 9–6 (5 in winter); Sun 9–12. Closed during
services 🚇 St.-Guidon/St.-Guido 🚻 Few 🎟 Free

ÉGLISE NOTRE-DAME DE LA CHAPELLE

Pieter Bruegel the Elder (➤ 56) was buried here,
close to the rue Haute, where he was born. A
memorial was erected by his son.
🚹 E8 ⊠ place de la Chapelle ☎ 02 513 5348 🕐 Summer:
Mon–Sat 9–5; Sun 1–3.30. Winter: Mon–Sat 11.30–4.30 🚇 Gare
Centrale/Centraal Station 🚌 20, 48 🚻 Good 🎟 Free

ÉGLISE NOTRE-DAME DE LAEKEN

This massive neo-Gothic church was commissioned
by Leopold I and designed by Joseph Poelaert in
1851. It is the burial place of the Belgian royal family.
🚹 E3 ⊠ parvis Notre Dame ☎ 02 478 2095 🕐 Guided tours Sun
2–5; services 1st Fri of month 5, Sat 5, Sun 9.15, 10.15, 11.30
🚇 Bockstael 🚻 Few 🎟 Free

ÉGLISE ST.-NICOLAS

Brussels' oldest church was founded in the 11th
century, but most of the interior dates from the 18th.
The curved building once followed the line of the
River Senne, and a cannonball in the wall recalls the
city's bombardment of 1695.
🚹 E7 ⊠ 1 rue au Beurre ☎ 02 513 8022 🕐 Mon–Sat 8–6.30;
Sun 9–7.35 🚇 Bourse/Beurs 🚌 29, 34, 47, 48, 60, 63, 65, 66, 71,
95, 96; tram 23, 52, 55, 56, 81 🚻 Good 🎟 Free

BRUGES

In the Top 25

🔲 **HEILIG BLOEDBASILIEK (➤ 50)**
🔲 **KATHEDRAAL ST.-SALVATOR (➤ 42)**
🔲 **ONZE-LIEVE-VROUWEKERK (➤ 45)**

JERUZALEMKERK

This 15th-century building was inspired by the Basilica
of the Holy Sepulchre in Jerusalem. Half of the 12
almshouses attached to the church have survived and
are now the Kantcentrum (lace centre, ➤ 72).
🚹 cIII ⊠ Peperstraat 3a ☎ 050 33 00 72 🕐 Mon–Fri 10–12,
2–6; Sat 10–1, 2–5. Closed hols 🚌 4, 6 🚻 Good 🎟 Inexpensive

SINT-WALBURGAKERK

Jesuit Pieter Huyssens built this splendid baroque
church between 1619 and 1642, and the 17th-century
oak pulpit is astonishing.
🚹 cIII ⊠ Sint-Maartensplein ☎ 050 34 32 57 🕐 Summer:
8–10PM and occasionally during the day. Winter: only during Sunday
services at 10, 7 🚌 6 🚻 None 🎟 Free

ST.-JAKOBSKERK

This beautiful church was
founded c1420 in a
neighbourhood of rich
Brugean families and foreign
delegations, who all made
generous donations for the
decoration of the building. The
church has an extremely rich
collection of paintings by
Pieter Pourbus, Lancelot
Blondeel, and several
anonymous Flemish
Primitives.
🚹 bIII ⊠ Moerstratt ☎ 050
33 18 34 🕐 July–Aug: daily
2–5.30. Sep–Jun: one hour
before mass on Sat from 3;
Sun from 11

Jeruzalemkerk

Architecture

BRUGEL AND ERASMUS

The 16th-century painter Pieter Bruegel the Elder was born in the Marolles (➤ 38) and his house at 132 rue Haute has been restored.
🕐 Wed, Sun 2–5 🚇 Louise
🎫 Inexpensive

The 16th-century humanist philosopher Erasmus spent five months in 1521 at 31 rue de Chapitre. This now contains a collection of documents by him and his contemporaries, as well as Renaissance furniture.
➕ F7 ☎ 02 521 1383
🕐 Wed, Thu, Sat–Mon 10–12, 2–5 🚇 St.-Guidon/St.-Guido

Art nouveau Old England

BOURSE

The Belgian Stock Exchange is in an elegant 1873 building with a decorative frieze by Albert-Ernest Carrier-Belleuse and sculptures by Auguste Rodin.
➕ E7 ✉ 2 rue H. Maus ☎ 02 509 1211 🕐 Mon–Fri for groups by prior arrangement 🚇 Bourse/Beurs 🚊 Tram 23, 52, 55, 56, 81
♿ Few 🎫 Free

EUROPEAN PARLIAMENT

The imposing facade of the European Parliament building, made of slick granite, glass, and steel, is nicknamed the *Caprice des Dieux* (whim of the gods). This is where the European Union's 626 members gather when in Brussels.
➕ G8 ✉ rue Wiertz ☎ 02 284 3457
🕐 Tours Mon–Thu 10, 3; Fri 3; Sat 10, 11.30, 2.30 🚇 Schuman 🎫 Free

GALERIES ST.-HUBERT

A covered arcade with new and old-fashioned stores, built in 1846–47, when this type of elegant shopping mall was a first in Europe.
➕ E7 ✉ rue du Marché-aux-Herbes
🚇 Gare Centrale/Centraal Station ♿ Good
🎫 Free

PALAIS DE JUSTICE

The Palais de Justice was one of Leopold II's pet projects, designed by Poelaert in grand eclectic style. The interior is as overwhelming as the views over Brussels from the terrace. The Palais de Justice still contains the main law courts.
➕ E8 ✉ place Poelaert ☎ 02 508 6578
🕐 Mon–Fri 9–3. Closed hols
🚇 Louise/Louiza 🚊 Tram 92, 93, 94
♿ Very good 🎫 Free

SERRES ROYALES (ROYAL GREENHOUSES)

Alphonse Balat and the young Victor Horta built this magnificent city of glass for Leopold II.

🚏 F2 ✉ 61 avenue du Parc Royal (Domaine Royal, Laeken) ☎ 02 513 8940 🕐 Only 2 weeks a year: end of Apr to May, when flowers are in bloom 🚇 Heysel/Heizel 🚊 53; tram 52, 92 🚻 Few 💷 Free during the day, moderate at night (details from tourist office)

THÉÂTRE DE LA MONNAIE

The original 1697 theatre was enlarged in 1819 by Napoleon to become one of the most beautiful in the world. It was here the Belgian Revolution began in August 1830. In 1985 the theatre was again enlarged, with a ceiling by Sam Francis and tiling by Sol Lewitt.

🚏 E7 ✉ place de la Monnaie
☎ Box office: 02 229 1211 (➤ 82) 🕐 Open during performances
🚇 De Brouckère 🚻 Very good

BRUGES

In the Top 25
- 🟦 BEGIJNHOF (➤ 43)
- 🟦 BURG (➤ 49)
- 🟦 GRUUTHUSE MUSEUM (➤ 46)
- 🟦 MARKT (➤ 48)
- 🟦 ST.-JANSHOSPITAAL (➤ 44)

CONCERTGEBOUW

Finished in 2002 to celebrate Bruges as the European City of Culture, this impressive structure has already become the city's fourth landmark. It has the largest stage in Belgium, and aims to attract top international performances.

🚏 BIII ✉ 't Zandt ☎ 050 47 69 99
🕐 During performances 🚊 2, 3,4, 8, 13, 15, 17, 25 💷 Free

SINT-JANSHUYSMOLEN

The only one of Bruges' four windmills that can be visited. It was built by a group of bakers in 1770 and was acquired by the city of Bruges in 1914. It still grinds grain. Inside is a museum.

🚏 cII ✉ Kruisvest 🕐 Thu–Tue 9.30–12.30, 1.30–5 🚊 4, 6,16
🚻 None 💷 Inexpensive

SEVEN WONDERS

The *Septem admirationes civitatis Brugensis* (Bruges' Seven Wonders) by P. Claessins the Elder (1499–1576), in the *Begijnhof* (➤ 43), depicts the Onze-Lieve-Vrouwekerk tower, the Halles and Belfry, as well as the House with the Seven Turrets. The Water Hall on the Markt, the Water House, and Hansa House no longer exist; only the tower of the Poorters' Lodge remains.

Bruges' Belfry

Attractions for Children

BRUSSELS FOR CHILDREN

Apart from parks and adventure parks, most activities for children happen indoors. Musée du Cinéma (➤ 84), Centre Belge de la Bande Dessinée (➤ 27), the musées d'Art Ancien et Moderne (➤ 33, 34) and the Musée Royal de l'Afrique Centrale (➤ 52–53) have workshops for children of various ages. For details see *The Bulletin* (➤ 24).

BRUSSELS

> **In the Top 25**
> 🟥 **AUTOWORLD (➤ 32)**
> 🟥 **CENTRE BELGE DE LA BANDE DESSINÉE (➤ 27)**
> 🟥 **MUSÉE ROYAL DE L'ARMÉE ET D'HISTOIRE MILITAIRE (➤ 32)**
> 🟥 **MUSÉE ROYAL D'ART ET D'HISTOIRE (➤ 32)**

BRUPARCK

Bruparck has a miniature Europe, with 350 models of monuments in the European Union. It also has a water funpark, Océade, and a huge cinema complex.
🟥 D2 ✉ 20 boulevard du Centenaire, Heysel ☎ 02 478 0550; www.minieurope.com 🕐 Varies with season and attraction 🚇 Heysel/Heizel 🔥 Good 💷 Very expensive

MUSÉE DES SCIENCES NATURELLES

This museum has one of the finest collections of whale skeletons in the world, dinosaurs in motion, birdspiders, and animals from around the world.
🟥 G8 ✉ 29 rue Wautier ☎ 02 627 4247 🕐 Tue–Fri 9.30–4.45; Sat–Sun 10–6 🚇 Trône/Troon 🚌 34, 80 💷 Moderate

Gaston Lagaffe/Guust Flater

SIX FLAGS BELGIUM

Spectacular theme park with gentle carousels, good rides, and a play area for children.
🟥 Off map ✉ Freeway E411 Brussels-Namur, exit 6, in Wavres/Waveren ☎ 010 42 15 00 🕐 May–Aug: daily 10–6. Sep: Sat–Sun 10–6 🚉 Train from Gare Schuman to Gare de Bierges on Ottignies/Louvain-la-Neuve line (short walk from station) 🔥 Few 💷 Very expensive

BRUGES

BOUDEWIJNPARK

The 30 attractions and shows here include an ice show and Europe's most sophisticated dolphinarium.
🟥 Off map ✉ avenue De Baeckestraat 12, St.-Michiels ☎ 050 38 38 38 🕐 Apr: daily 11–5. May, Jun: daily 10.30–5. Jul, Aug: daily 10–6. At other times of the year call ahead to check the park is open 🚌 7, 17 from railway station 🔥 Good 💷 Very expensive

DE ZEVEN TORENTJES (CHILDREN'S FARM)

This former 14th-century feudal estate with an authentic pigeon-house and gothic barn is now a children's farm with a fine playground.
🟥 Off map ✉ Canadaring 41, Assebroek ☎ 050 35 40 43 🕐 Mon–Fri 8.30–noon, 2–4 🚌 2

Parks

BOIS DE LA CAMBRE

Once part of the Forest of Soignes, the Bois was annexed by the city in 1862 and laid out by landscape artist Keilig. Boating, fishing, and roller-skating.

➕ G11–G12 ✉ Main entrance on avenue Louise
🕐 Dawn–dusk 🚊 Tram 93, 94 ♿ Few 💵 Free

FORÊT DE SOIGNES

A wonderful beech forest that includes Tervuren Arboretum (☎ 02 769 2081), Groenendaal Arboretum (☎ 02 657 0386), and Jean Massart Experimental Garden.

➕ G13–H13–J13–K13 ✉ Boitsfort ☎ 02 629
3411/660 6417 🕐 Guided tours Thu and Sun at 10.30
🍴 Restaurant 🚊 Tram 34, 44 ♿ None 💵 Free

PARC DE LAEKEN

Enough to amuse you all day. Beyond its attractive lawns lie the Royal Residence and the amazing Royal Greenhouses (➤ 57).

➕ E2 ✉ Main entrance on boulevard de Smet de Naeyer, Laeken
🕐 Dawn–dusk 🚇 Heysel/Heizel 🚊 Tram 23 ♿ Few 💵 Free

BRUGES

KONINGIN ASTRIDPARK

Laid out in 18th-century English-country style, with a good children's playground.

➕ dlll ✉ Main entrance Park 🕐 24 hours 🚌 1, 11
♿ Good 💵 Free

MINNEWATERPARK

On the edge of Lake Minnewater, with a sculpture garden and free concerts in summer.

➕ blV ✉ Arsenaalstraat 🕐 Dawn–dusk 🍴 Café-restaurant
🚌 All buses to the train station ♿ Good 💵 Free

TILLEGEMBOS

Well-kept woodland with footpaths, playground, picnic areas, horse-mill, and a charming rural inn, De Trutselaar, serving snacks, pancakes, or waffles.

➕ Off map ✉ Torhoutse steenweg, St.-Michiels ☎ 050 38 02 96
🕐 Daily dawn–dusk 💵 Free 🚌 25

parc de Bruxelles

BRUSSELS' GREEN SPACES

Parks cover nearly 14 percent of Brussels and provide an extremely high ratio of green space per inhabitant (27.5sq-m/296sq-ft). The parks in the centre, although well laid out, often feel charmingly unkempt and abandoned, particularly on weekends, when most people head for the woods and other green spaces just outside the city.

Markets in Brussels

MARKETS IN BRUGES

The weekly market on the 't'Zand attracts large crowds every Saturday morning. Goods for sale range from clothes to household products, music, and farm-made goat's cheese. On the nearby Beursplein, stands sell fruit, vegetables, and flowers. A smaller food and flower market is held on the Markt (► 48) on Wednesday mornings. On Saturday and Sunday mornings from March to October there is an antiques and secondhand market on the Dijver and Vismarkt.

An antique market in Le Sablon

GARE DU MIDI

The Marché du Midi is one of Europe's largest, with fresh fruit and vegetables, fish, meat, clothes, pictures, household goods, North African music, and books.
✚ D8 ⊠ Near the Gare du Midi ⏰ Sun 7–1 🚇 Gare du Midi/Zuidstation 🚋 Tram 23, 52, 55, 56, 81, 82, 90 ♿ Few 🎫 Free

GRAND' PLACE

Small flower and plant market.
✚ E7 ⊠ Grand' Place ⏰ Daily 8–6 🚇 Bourse/Beurs 🚋 Tram 23, 52, 55, 56, 81 ♿ Good 🎫 Free

PLACE DU CHÂTELAIN

Popular evening market in Ixelles, with stands selling fruit and vegetables, breads, cheeses, and charcuterie.
✚ F9 ⊠ place du Châtelain ⏰ Wed 2–7, or later 🚋 Tram 81

PLACE DE LA DUCHESSE DE BRABANT

The Brabant Province around Brussels is renowned for its strong horses, still used as draught horses on many Belgian farms. These beautiful animals, as well as racehorses, are sold here after much bargaining.
✚ C7–D7 ⊠ place de la Duchesse de Brabant ⏰ Tue 8–1 🚇 Gare de l'Ouest/Weststation 🚋 63, 89 ♿ Few 🎫 Free

PLACE DU GRAND SABLON

The place du Grand Sablon is crowded with antique shops, but on weekends there is a small street market full of collectables. Don't expect bargains!
✚ E8 ⊠ place du Grand Sablon ⏰ Sat 9–6; Sun 9–2 🚋 48; tram 91, 92, 93, 94 ♿ Few 🎫 Free

PLACE DU JEU DE BALLE

Sunday is definitely the best day to browse around this great junk market in Les Marolles district. Arrive early for bargains.
✚ E8 ⊠ place du Jeu de Balle ⏰ Daily 7–2 🚋 48 ♿ Good 🎫 Free

Canals in Bruges

Bruges is often referred to as "the Venice of the North" and its *reien* (as the Flemish call their canals) provide much of its romantic charm. Taking a boat on the canals is one of the best ways to explore the heart of the city. Except when the canals are frozen, there are daily guided tours in several languages, including English. Illuminated evening tours, offered in summer, are especially pleasant.

Canal along the Dijver

AUGUSTIJNENREI

One of the less spectacular canals, but nonetheless beautiful, with the Augustijnen Bridge (*c*1425) and the adjacent Spaanse Loskaai road, whose name recalls Spanish presence in the 14th and 15th centuries.

 bll 🚃 3

DIJVER

The lovely little walkway along this canal shows off some of Bruges' grandest architecture: At No. 11 is the College of Europe, at No. 12 is the Groeninge Museum (➤ 47), and at No. 17 is the Gruuthuse Museum (➤ 46). In the summer there is a Saturday and Sunday junk market.

🚻 blll 🚃 1, 6, 11, 16

GROENEREI/STEENHOUWERSDIJK

The view of this canal from the Vismarkt (Fish Market) is one of the most idyllic (and often-painted) in Bruges. The Meebrug and the Peerdenbrug are two of Bruges' oldest stone bridges. At the end of the Groenerei is the almshouse De Pelikaan (1634), which is well worth a visit.

🚻 dll 🚃 1, 6, 11, 16

ROZENHOEDKAAI

Another wonderful corner, with rear views of the buildings of the Burg and the Huidenvettersplein, and of the famous Duc de Bourgogne Hotel.

🚻 blll 🚃 1, 6, 11, 16

MINNEWATER

Lying to the south of Walplein and Wijngaarrdplein is the Minnewater or Lake of Love, which was the outer harbour of Bruges before the river silted up, cutting the city off from the sea. The lake is named after a woman called Minna who, according to legend, fell in love with a man her father did not approve of. Desolate Minna hid in the woods around the lake, where she died before her lover could rescue her. Her lover parted the waters and buried her beneath the lake.

Festivals & Processions

MEIBOOM (RAISING OF THE MAYPOLE)

On 9 August, a procession from the Sablon (➤ 37) to

Ommegang *procession*

the Grand' Place (➤ 30) recalls an attack on a wedding party in 1213 by bandits from Leuven. The gang was foiled and the grateful duke allowed the party to plant a *meiboom*, or maypole, on their saint's feast day.

OMMEGANG

On the first Tuesday and Thursday in July, this colourful procession (literally "doing the rounds") goes from the place du Grand Sablon (➤ 37) to the Grand' Place (➤ 30). Dating back to the 14th century, it celebrates

the arrival of a statue of the Virgin from Antwerp. Nowadays it ends in a dance on the illuminated Grand' Place from 9PM to midnight. Dance tickets, available from late May, are expensive and must be reserved in advance with the Brussels Tourist Office (✉ Town Hall, Grand' Place, 1000 Brussels ☎ 02 513 8940; fax 02 514 4538).

CARNIVAL

Several Belgian cities, including Brussels and Bruges, celebrate Carnival around mid-February, with a procession and the election of the Carnival Prince. The main event is on Shrove Tuesday, Mardi Gras, when people dressed in richly embroidered costumes and masks dance in the cities' main squares to ward off evil spirits (information from the tourist offices, ➤ 91).

GOUDEN BOOMSTOET (PAGEANT OF THE GOLDEN TREE)

This magnificent procession, held in August–September 2002 and every five years thereafter, re-enacts the festivities for the wedding of Charles the Bold and Margaret of York, celebrated in Bruges.

HEILIG BLOEDKAPEL PROCESSION

Every year at 3PM on Ascension Day (May) the relic of the Holy Blood (➤ 50) is taken out in a spectacular procession involving thousands of people. Scenes in the procession tell stories from the Bible, as well as the legend of the coming of the Holy Blood to Bruges and the worship of the relic. Information from Bruges Tourist Office (✉ Burg 11 ☎ 050 44 86 86).

BRUSSELS & BRUGES
where to

Belgium's Best Dining

PRICES

Expect to pay the following per person for a three-course meal without drinks:

€€€ over €45
€€ €20–€45
€ under €20

THE KING OF BELGIAN FOOD

Pierre Wynants, owner and chef of the famous Comme chez Soi restaurant (▶ this page) is an authority on Belgian and other European food. He has transformed Belgium's cuisine and has put traditional ingredients like Belgian beer and hop shoots on his menus.

BRUSSELS

LA BELLE MARAÎCHÈRE (€€–€€€)

Well-known traditional fish restaurant on Brussels' old harbour. The *waterzooi* (fish stew) is excellent and set menus are great value.

🔛 E7 ✉ 11 place Ste.-Catherine, Ste.-Catherine ☎ 02 512 9759 🕓 Fri–Tue lunch, dinner 🚇 Ste.-Catherine/St. Katelijne 🚋 Tram 23, 52, 55, 56, 81, 90

BRUNEAU (€€€)

Traditional Belgian food at its very best in a sumptuous setting, with three Michelin stars. Dishes include ravioli with celery and truffles, and crusty duck breast.

🔛 C5 ✉ 73–75 avenue Broustin, Ganshoren ☎ 02 427 6978 🕓 Thu–Mon lunch, dinner 🚇 Basilique

CHEZ MARIE (€€–€€€)

This trendy restaurant serves delectable French-Belgian food. The wine list is one of the city's finest and the two-course lunch is good value.

🔛 G9 ✉ 40 rue Alphonse de Witte, Ixelles ☎ 02 644 3031 🕓 Mon–Fri lunch, dinner; Sat dinner 🚌 71, 36; tram 81

COMME CHEZ SOI (€€€)

By common consent Belgium's finest restaurant (quite something in a country with so many fine restaurants), with dishes such as sweetbreads with hop shoots and sole fillets with Riesling mousseline and shrimp. You need to book weeks ahead as there are only 40 seats.

🔛 E7 ✉ 23 place Rouppe, centre ☎ 02 512 2921 🕓 Tue–Sat lunch, dinner. Closed Jul 🚇 Anneessens 🚋 Tram 23, 52, 55, 56, 81

L'ECAILLER DU PALAIS ROYAL (€€€)

The perfect place to take a Belgian minister or banker. The decor is stuffy and bourgeois, the clientele serious and respectable, and the food always impeccable, with excellent *croquettes aux crevettes* (shrimp croquettes) and Zeeland oysters. Book a week ahead.

🔛 E8 ✉ 18 rue Bodenbroeck, Sablon ☎ 02 512 8751 🕓 Mon–Sat lunch, dinner. Closed Aug 🚋 34, 95, 96; tram 92, 93, 94

LA MAISON DU CYGNE (€€€)

Dine on scrumptious truffles, rich mousses, and *foie gras* in this luxurious restaurant with great views of the Grand' Place. Go with an empty stomach and a full wallet.

🔛 E7 ✉ 9 Grand' Place, centre ☎ 02 511 8244 🕓 Mon–Fri lunch, dinner; Sat dinner only 🚇 Gare Centrale/Centraal Station

LA MANUFACTURE (€€)

This modern restaurant in the old Delvaux leather factory serves delicious and inventive European food with a touch of Asia. Courtyard tables in summer.

🔛 D7 ✉ 12 rue Notre-Dame du Sommeil, centre ☎ 02 502 2525 🕓 Mon–Fri lunch, dinner; Sat dinner 🚇 Bourse/Beurs 🚋 Tram 23, 52, 55, 56, 81, 90

LA QUINCAILLERIE (€€€)

An elegant and delightful restaurant in an old hardware store, a short walk from the Horta Museum (► 40). La Quincaillerie specializes in fish and seafood, serving huge platters of seafood, but you'll also find other delights of the Belgian and French kitchen.

✚ F10 ⊠ rue du Page 45, Ixelles/Elsene ☎ 02 538 2553 ⓘ Mon–Fri lunch, dinner; weekend dinner only 🚌 54; tram 81

BRUGES

DEN BRAAMBERG (€€€)

Award-winning Belgian-French cuisine prepared by chef François Bogaert, who does amazing things with fish and lamb. The setting is lavish, and typically Flemish, in a beautiful 18th-century patrician house.

✚ b–cIII ⊠ 11 Pandreitje ☎ 050 33 73 70 ⓘ Mon, Wed–Sat lunch, dinner 🚌 6, 16

DEN GOUDEN HARYNCK (€€–€€€)

The fine chef in this typically Brugean restaurant prepares the freshest ingredients without too many frills. Dishes include pleasant surprises like smoked lobster with fig chutney and scallops with goose liver.

✚ bIII ⊠ Groeninge 25 ☎ 050 33 76 37 ⓘ Tues–Sat lunch, dinner 🚌 1

DE KARMELIET (€€€)

Often regarded as Bruges' best restaurant, De Karmeliet serves the inspired Belgian cuisine of Geert Van Hecke in a stylish mansion with outside terrace.

✚ cIII ⊠ Langestraat 19 ☎ 050 33 82 59 ⓘ Mon–Sat lunch, dinner; Sun lunch

'T PANDREITJE (€€€)

The fish is excellent in this much-lauded restaurant, particularly the smoked eel pie and fresh seafood. There are several *dégustation* menus as well as à la carte dishes, and the setting is comfortably plush, with service in the lovely garden in summer.

✚ cIII ⊠ Pandreitje 6 ☎ 050 33 11 90 ⓘ Mon, Tue, Thu–Sat lunch, dinner 🚌 1, 6, 11, 16

PATRICK DEVOS "DE ZILVEREN PAUW" (€€€)

This celebrated restaurant in a stylish house with art nouveau decor serves light and inventive Belgian-French cuisine.

✚ bIII ⊠ Zilverstraat 41, central ☎ 050 33 55 66 ⓘ Mon–Fri lunch, dinner; Sat dinner 🚌 All buses

DE SNIPPE (€€€)

At this popular restaurant in an 18th-century house, Luc Huysentruyt, disciple of Auguste Escoffier, the late chef and author, displays his flair both for innovation and tradition.

✚ cIII ⊠ Nieuwe Gentweg 53 ☎ 050 33 70 70 ⓘ Tue–Sat lunch, dinner; Sun, Mon dinner 🚌 1, 11

BRUGES ANNO 1468

Celebrate the wedding anniversary (3 July 1468) of Charles the Bold and Margaretha of York with a gigantic four-course dinner. Beer and wine flow, and minstrels, knights, dancers, and fire eaters entertain. Reservations esssential. ⊠ Vlamingstraat 84, 8000 Bruges ☎ 050 34 75 72; www.proximedia.com/web/celebentert.html ⓘ Apr–Oct: Thu, Fri, Sat 7.30PM. Nov–Mar: Sat only

Brasseries & *Fritures*

FRITES, FRITES, FRITES...

Belgium claims the best fries in the world. The secret of their *frites* is that they are fried twice and thrown in the air to get rid of the extra oil. Every Belgian has a favourite *friture* or *frietkot*, but most agree that Friture Ste.-Catherine, on place Ste.-Catherine, and La Barrière St.-Gilles, 3 Chaussée d'Alsemberg, in St. Gilles, are among the best.

BRUSSELS

L'AMADEUS (€€)

A romantic wine bar/restaurant in the former studio of the sculptor Auguste Rodin. This is a popular hang-out for the sophisticated Ixelles crowd, particularly for Sunday brunch. Excellent wine list and an extensive menu of modern and more traditional Belgian dishes.
➕ E/F9 ✉ 13 rue Veydt, Ixelles ☎ 02 538 3427 🕐 Tue–Sun noon–1AM; Mon 6.30PM–2AM. Closed Aug 🚇 Louise

AU STEKERLAPATTE (€)

This dark maze of a restaurant serves a long menu of traditional Belgian dishes—among them *poularde de Bruxelles au champignons* (chicken with mushrooms) and excellent steak tartare. With its friendly service and a good atmosphere, it draws other restaurateurs on their day off.
➕ E8 ✉ 4 rue des Prêtres ☎ 02 512 8681 🕐 Tue–Sun dinner 🚇 Hôtel des Monnaies/Munthof

BISTRO M'ALAIN DE LA MER (€€)

A relaxed and friendly bistro with great Belgian-French food, specializing in fish and seafood (the chef is from Brittany). Those who prefer meat have a choice of dishes, from goose liver to quail or pigeon. Good value.
➕ E7 ✉ place St.-Catherine 15, Ste.-Catherine ☎ 02 217 9012 🕐 Thu–Mon lunch, dinner 🚇 Ste.-Catherine/St. Katelijne

IN 'T SPINNEKOPKE (€€)

This rustic restaurant serves Belgian dishes such as *waterzooi* and rabbit cooked in *gueuze* beer.
➕ E7 ✉ 1 place Jardin aux Fleurs ☎ 02 511 8695 🕐 Sun–Fri lunch, dinner; Sat dinner 🚇 Ste. Catherine/St. Katelijine or Bourse/Beurs

LE PAIN QUOTIDIEN/HET DAGELYJKS BROOD (€)

In this chain of tea rooms, breakfast, lunch, snacks, and afternoon tea are served around one big table. The breads, croissants, pastries, and jams are all homemade.
➕ E8 ✉ 11 rue des Sablons ☎ 02 513 5154 🕐 7.30–7 🚍 4, 95; tram 20, 48
➕ E7 ✉ 16 Rue Antoine Dansaert ☎ 02 502 2361

LE PETIT BOXEUR (€€)

Quaint restaurant with candles and jazz music, serving traditional Belgian fare, as well as more creative dishes.
➕ E7 ✉ 3 rue Borgval, Ste.-Catherine ☎ 02 511 4000 🕐 Tue–Sun 7.30PM–12.30AM 🚇 Bourse/Beurs

TAVERNE DU PASSAGE (€–€€)

This elegant brasserie, founded in 1928, is known for its *croquettes au crevettes* (shrimp croquettes) and traditional Brussels cuisine. The *choucroute au jambon* (saurerkraut with ham) is a must.
➕ E7 ✉ 30 Galerie de la Reine ☎ 02 512 3732 🕐 Daily noon–midnight 🚇 Gare Centrale/Centraal Station

DE ULTIEME HALLUCINATIE (€€)

This is worth a visit just for the splendid art nouveau interior, but the French food also lives up to expectation. The goose- and duck-liver dishes and poached fish in *gueuze* sauce are delicious. Popular café.

⊞ F6 ✉ 316 rue Royale ☎ 02 217 0614 ⏰ Mon–Fri lunch, dinner; Sat 5PM–3AM Ⓠ Botanique/Kruidtuin

BRUGES

CAFEDRAAL (€€)

Hidden seafood restaurant where you'll find *waterzooi* and an excellent North Sea bouillabaisse. Beautiful torchlit garden terrace.

⊞ bIII ✉ Zilverstraat 38 ☎ 050 34 08 45 ⏰ Tue–Sat lunch, dinner 🚌 1, 2, 3, 4, 5, 8, 9, 11, 13, 16

CHEZ OLIVIER (€€)

This homey place is in an old house with fine views over one of the prettiest canals, and the French fare is simple but stylish.

⊞ cIII ✉ Meestraat 9 ☎ 050 33 36 59 ⏰ Mon–Fri lunch, dinner; Sat dinner. Jun–Aug: closed lunch 🚌 6, 16

DEN DIJVER (€€)

All dishes here, both meat and fish, are lovingly prepared with Belgian beer. The interior is old Flemish, and the view from the summer terrace is tops.

⊞ bIII ✉ Dijver 5 ☎ 050 33 60 69 ⏰ Fri–Tue lunch, dinner; Wed, Thu dinner 🚌 1, 6, 11, 16

DE FLORENTIJNEN (€€–€€€)

Mouth-watering modern, light French dishes with a flavour of Italy are served in this much talked about, charming restaurant, in an imposing corner house with high ceilings. Try the pigeon with truffle gravy, or lobster with glacé garlic.

⊞ bIII ✉ Academiestraat 1 ☎ 050 67 75 33 ⏰ Tue–Sat lunch, dinner; Sun lunch 🚌 4

HET DAGELIJKS BROOD (€)

Excellent snacks throughout the day.

⊞ bIII ✉ Philip Stockstraat 21 ☎ 050 33 60 50/050 33 67 66 ⏰ Mon, Wed–Sat 7–6; Sun 8–6 🚌 All buses

IN DEN WITTEKOP (€€)

A characterful, family-run *eetkroeg* or "bar where you can eat," specializing in regional Belgian dishes. The *carbonnades flamandes* (beef stewed in beer) and fish soup are particularly good here, but the more adventurous may want to try the goose liver with apple and *peperkoek*.

⊞ bIII ✉ Sint Jacobstraat 14 ☎ 050 33 20 59 ⏰ Tue–Sat lunch, dinner 🚌 3, 13

SIPHON (€€)

This popular restaurant outside Bruges serves Flemish dishes such as river eel in green herb sauce and grilled T-bone steaks. Good value. Book well ahead.

⊞ Off map ✉ Damse Vaart Oost 1 ☎ 050 62 02 02 ⏰ Sat–Wed lunch, dinner 🚌 1.5km (1 mile) from Damme (▶ 21)

BELGIAN DISHES

There is more to Belgian food than *moules frites*. *Waterzooi* is a little-known national dish, a delicate green stew of fish or chicken with leeks, parsley, and cream. Plain but delicious, *stoemp* is potatoes mashed with vegetables, often served with sausages. *Carbonnade flamande* is beef braised in beer with carrots and thyme, and *lapin à la gueuze* is rabbit stewed in *gueuze* beer with prunes. *Anguilles au vert/ paling in het groen* (river eels in green sauce) is another popular dish. A real treat are Belgian waffles on sale in the streets or in tea rooms, eaten with icing sugar, whipped cream, or fruit.

International Cuisine

STREET OF THE WORLD

The rue Antoine Dansaert, in Brussels, has a wide variety of ethnic restaurants in different price ranges. Young Bruxellois often choose the inexpensive Vietnamese Da Kao at No. 38 for a quick bite to eat, while the trendy crowd heads for the contemporary Mediterranean cuisine of Bonsoir Clara at No. 22. Next door are Kasbah (► this page) and Neos Cosmos (► 69).

BRUSSELS

ATELIER DE LA GRANDE ÎLE (€€)

Set in an old foundry, this Russian restaurant serves hearty meat dishes and a long list of vodkas, all accompanied by live gypsy music. The atmosphere is joyous, sometimes electric.
🔢 E7 ✉ rue de la Grande île 33 ☎ 02 512 8190 🕐 Tue–Sun 8PM–1AM. Closed Aug 🚇 Bourse/Beurs

AU THÉ DE PEKIN (€)

Hong Kong cuisine and some Far Eastern fare are served in this simple room. Very good value.
🔢 E7 ✉ 16–24 rue de la Vierge Noire, Central ☎ 02 513 4642 🕐 Daily lunch, dinner 🚇 Bourse/Beurs

LES BAGUETTES IMPERIALES (€€€)

Belgium's best Asian restaurant, with refined Vietnamese dishes.
🔢 D2–D3 ✉ 70 avenue Jean Sobieski ☎ 02 479 6732 🕐 Mon, Wed–Sat lunch, dinner; Sun lunch 🚇 Stuyvenbergh 🚌 19, 23

BENI ZNASSEN–CHEZ MUSTAPHA (€–€€)

The most authentic Moroccan restaurant in town, offering the ultimate couscous. The decor is unassuming but that is part of its charm.
🔢 D–E9 ✉ 81 rue de l'Eglise, St.-Gilles ☎ 02 534 1194 🕐 Wed–Sun dinner. Closed Jul, Aug 🚇 Parvis St.-Gilles

CASTELLO BANJI (€€)

Excellent art nouveau Italian restaurant. Try the delicious beef *carpaccio*

with truffles in season and spinach lasagne.
🔢 E8 ✉ 12 rue Bodenbroek ☎ 02 512 8794 🕐 Tue–Sat lunch, dinner 🚌 20, 48; tram 91, 92, 93, 94

CHEZ FATMA (€–€€)

Fatma and Fergani Loussaifi, the king and queen of couscous, preside over the city's favourite Tunisian restaurant.
🔢 G8 ✉ 18 place Jourdan ☎ 02 230 9597 🕐 Mon–Fri lunch, dinner; Sat dinner 🚌 80

GIOCONDA STORE CONVIVIO (€–€€)

A lively restaurant attached to an Italian wine and delicatessen store, serving tasty pasta dishes. A great place for lunch or an easy-going evening meal. The waiters are friendly and entertaining.
🔢 E–F9–10 ✉ rue de l'Aqueduc 76, Ixelles ☎ 02 539 3299 🕐 Mon–Sat lunch, dinner 🚌 54; tram 81

KASBAH, RESTAURANT & SALON (€€)

A delightful dark blue cave of a place, this popular Moroccan restaurant surprises with its large menu of *tajines* (stew cooked in an earthenware pot), couscous, and grills accompanied by Arabic music. The Sunday brunch is excellent and a very good value.
🔢 E7 ✉ 20 rue Antoine Dansaert, Central ☎ 02 502 4026 🕐 Daily lunch, dinner; Sat dinner 🚇 Bourse/Beurs 🚌 Tram 23, 52, 55, 56, 81

NEOS COSMOS (€€)

Lively, refined Greek restaurant serving excellent *meze* in an attractive, contemporary setting.

➕ E7 ✉ 50 rue Antoine Dansaert, Central ☎ 02 511 8058 ⏰ Mon–Fri lunch, dinner; Sat dinner 🚇 Bourse/Beurs 🚊 Tram 23, 52, 55, 56, 81

Ô-CHINOISE-RIZ (€–€€)

Very good, inexpensive Chinese restaurant, frequented mainly by the city's Chinese community. The food is therefore authentic and you can enjoy the spectacle of the food being prepared in the open-plan kitchen.

➕ E–F9–10 ✉ rue de l'Aqueduc 94, Ixelles ☎ 02 534 9108 ⏰ Mon–Fri lunch, dinner; Sat, Sun dinner 🚇 Hôtel des Monnaies 🚊 54; tram 81

TAGAWA (€€€)

The best Japanese food in Brussels in a very Asian setting. The sushi is divine and other dishes are prepared by the chefs at your table, but the pleasure is not inexpensive.

➕ F10 ✉ 279 Avenue Louise, Ixelles ☎ 02 640 5095 ⏰ Mon–Fri lunch, dinner; Sat dinner only 🚇 Louise 🚊 Tram 94

BRUGES

BHAVANI (€€)

Bruges' best Indian restaurant specializes in tandoori and vegetarian dishes.

➕ blll ✉ Simon Stevinplein 5 ☎ 050 33 90 25 ⏰ Daily lunch, dinner 🚌 All buses

BODEGA LORENA (€€)

Senor Rodrigues, the master of *tapas*, serves more than 60 types here.

➕ blll ✉ Loppemstraat 13 ☎ 050 34 88 17 ⏰ Tue–Sat dinner 🚌 All buses

CASABLANCA (€€)

Homey Moroccan restaurant where two ladies, Samira and Warda, prepare the delicious tagines and a choice of couscous dishes.

➕ b–clV ✉ Katelijnestraat 139 ☎ 050 61 14 77 ⏰ Wed–Mon lunch, dinner 🚌 Bus 1, 11

DE LANGE MUUR (€–€€)

This restaurant serves Canton, Fukien, and Peking food, and is renowned for its Chinese fondue and *rijsttafels* (spicy dishes with plain rice).

➕ blll ✉ St.-Amandsplein 11 ☎ 050 33 27 19 ⏰ Daily lunch, dinner 🚌 All buses

TANUKI (€€)

Classic Japanese dishes in an authentic setting with plenty of wood, a rock-tiled floor, and a bamboo garden. Excellent sushi and tempura.

➕ blV ✉ Oude Gentweg 1 ☎ 050 34 75 12 ⏰ Wed–Sun lunch, dinner 🚌 1, 11

TRIUM (€)

Bruges' best Italian restaurant serves fresh homemade pasta and crunchy pizzas. The waiters are some of the most charming outside Italy.

➕ blll ✉ Academiestraat 23 ☎ 050 33 30 60 ⏰ Tue–Sun 9–9 🚌 4

VEGETARIAN CHOICE

Belgians like their meat, but it should not be too difficult for vegetarians to find something to eat. There is always plenty of fish on the menu, and salads are an increasingly popular choice for lunch. Vegetarians will also find plenty of vegetable dishes in the ethnic restaurants, as well as in some specifically vegetarian restaurants. In Brussels there are Dolma (✉ 331 chaussée d'Ixelles ☎ 02 649 8981) and La Tsampa (✉ 109 rue de Livourne, Ixelles ☎ 02 647 0367), two Tibetan health food restaurants. In Bruges, head for the organic De Lotus (✉ 5 Wapenmakersstraat ✉ 050 33 10 78).

Bars & Cafés

A GLASS OF BEER

There are more than 400 varieties of Belgian beer. *Lambic* is a beer that ferments spontaneously; the yeast for its fermentation is not added by the brewer but is that found naturally in the local air. *Gueuze* is a mixture of *lambics*, while sweet *kriek* is *lambic* with cherries. Trappist beers come as *doubels* with 6–7 percent alcohol or *tripels* at 8 or 9 percent. Refreshing and lighter is *bierre blanche* or *witbier*, made of wheat and often drunk with a slice of lemon. Many of these beers come with their own glasses, specially designed to make the most of the beer's flavour and perfume. In the café La Lunette on the place de la Monnaie, every "lunette" comes in a one-litre *coupe* (like an outsized champagne glass). In winter Belgians like to have a tiny glass of *jenever*, a popular local spirit similar to gin—guaranteed to warm you up!

BRUSSELS

A LA MORT SUBITE

This traditional bar was once among singer Jacques Brel's favourite watering holes and is still popular. It even has its own brew, called *Mort Subite* (Sudden Death) because of its higher alcohol content.
➕ E7 ✉ 7 rue Montagne aux Herbes Potagères ☎ 02 513 1318 🕐 Daily 11AM–1AM 🚇 Gare Centrale/Centraal station

L'ACROBAT

Kitschy bar full of plastic roses, madonnas, and bright colours. Frequent live concerts and dancing in the back after midnight.
➕ E7 ✉ 14 rue Borgval, Ste.-Catherine ☎ 02 513 7308 🕐 Daily 9PM–dawn. Dance floor Fri, Sat 🚇 Bourse/Beurs 🚊 Tram 23, 52, 55, 56, 81, 90

L'ARCHIDUC

Funky, smoky Art Deco lounge designed like a cruise ship. It still looks the same as when it first opened in the 1930s, and they only play jazz or thirties music, but the crowd is spot on.
➕ E7 ✉ 6 rue Antoine Dansaert, Ste.-Catherine ☎ 02 512 0652 🕐 Daily 4PM–6AM 🚇 Bourse/Beurs

AU SOLEIL

Popular bar in a former old-fashioned men's clothing shop. Tables outside in summer.
➕ E7 ✉ 86 rue du Marché au Charbon ☎ 02 513 3430 🕐 Daily 10AM–2.30AM 🚇 Bourse/Beurs 🚊 Tram 23, 52, 55, 56, 81, 90

LE FALSTAFF

At some time during an evening out everyone usually ends up at this huge but always busy art deco café with a vast terrace that's heated in winter.
➕ E7 ✉ 17–23 rue Henri Maus ☎ 02 511 9877 🕐 Sun–Thu 11.30AM–2AM; Fri, Sat 11.30AM–4AM 🚇 Bourse/Beurs 🚊 Tram 23, 52, 55, 56, 81, 90

LE JAVA

Small, noisy bar—the perfect place to end a night on the town.
➕ E7 ✉ 31 rue St.-Géry ☎ 02 512 3716 🕐 Mon–Sat 8PM–3AM; Sun noon–3AM 🚇 Bourse/Beurs 🚊 Tram 23, 52, 55, 56, 81, 90

LE ROY D'ESPAGNE

Popular with tourists and Bruxellois alike, this large café-restaurant is particularly recommended for having an apéritif on the terrace or a drink on its upper floor, for the best views on this gorgeous square. If it was good enough for Karl Marx and Engels…
➕ E7 ✉ Grand' Place 1 ☎ 02 513 0807 🕐 Daily 10AM–1AM 🚇 Bourse/Beurs or Gare Centrale/Centraal station

T'WARM WATER

Authentic Bruxellois café where you can have a healthy breakfast or typical Bruxellois food, as well as artisanal *lambic* beer. They often have performances in the now rare Bruxellois dialect.
➕ E8 ✉ 19 rue des Renards, Marolles ☎ 02 513 9159 🕐 Daily 8AM–7PM 🚊 20, 48

DE ULTIEME HALLUCINATIE (► 67)

ZEBRA

Simple red-brick walls, outdoor terrace, and good music, Zebra is in a lively and popular nightlife area.

🔢 E7 ✉ 33 place St.-Géry
☎ 02 511 0901 🕐 7.30AM–1AM or later Ⓜ Bourse/Beurs
🚊 Tram 23, 52, 55, 56, 81

BRUGES

BISTRO DU PHARE

Popular hang-out for locals serving a large variety of Belgian beers and fresh snacks. There is a pleasant garden terrace in summer.

🔢 cll ✉ Sasplein 2 ☎ 050 34 35 90 🕐 Mon–Sat 10AM–2AM 🚌 4

'T BRUGS BEERTJE

The place for true beer lovers, with 300 traditionally brewed Belgian beers—many of them rare and for sale only here and all served in their special glass. The atmosphere is as Belgian as can be, and the bartender is always happy to help you choose a beer.

🔢 blll ✉ Kemelstraat 5
☎ 050 33 96 16 🕐 Thu–Tue 4PM–1AM 🚌 All buses

L'ESTAMINET

Intimate café with a good snack menu. The spaghetti bolognese is legendary. The busy summer terrace overlooks the park.

🔢 clll ✉ park 5, across from Astrid Park ☎ 050 33 09 16
🕐 Tue, Wed, Fri–Sun 11AM until last customer leaves; Mon afternoon 🚌 All buses to the Markt

DE GARRE

In tiny alley between the Burg and Markt, this 16th-century bar has a huge selection of Belgian beers. Plays classical music.

🔢 blll ✉ De Garre 1
☎ 050 34 10 29 🕐 Mon–Thu noon–midnight; Fri–Sun noon–1AM 🚌 All buses

DE LOKKEDIZE

This popular candle-lit jazz café is often full, although the noisiest tipplers stay around the bar. Light snacks.

🔢 blll ✉ Korte Vulderstraat 33 ☎ 050 33 44 50
🕐 Tue–Thu 7PM–3AM; Fri–Sun 6PM–3AM or later 🚌 4, 8

OU DE VLISSINGHE

Reputedly the oldest café in Bruges, built around 1515, this is popular with locals as well as visitors. Relaxed and easy-going.

🔢 clll ✉ Blekerstraat 2
☎ 050 34 37 37 🕐 Wed–Sat 11AM–midnight or later; Sun 11AM–8PM 🚌 4, 8

DE REPUBLIEK (CACTUS CLUB)

Large and hugely popular bar next to the cultural venue of the Cactus Club. High ceilings, a garden in summer, and a good selection of beers and snacks.

🔢 blll ✉ St.-Jacobsstraat 33
☎ 050 34 02 29 🕐 Daily 11AM–1AM or later 🚌 All buses

DE TOP

This tiny bar gets livelier as the night goes on and has an eclectic young crowd.

🔢 blll ✉ St.-Salvatorskerkhof 5 ☎ 050 33 03 51 🕐 Thu–Sun 9PM–dawn 🚌 All buses

BEER IN BRUGES

There are two breweries in the town centre. De Gouden Boom (✉ Verbrand Nieuwland ☎ 050 33 06 99) makes *Tarwebier*, a wheat beer that's good with a slice of lemon, and a stronger brew called *Brugse Tripel* with a 9.5 percent alcohol content. De Straffe Hendrik (✉ Walplein 26 ☎ 050 33 26 97) brews another wheat beer with a sweet aroma.

Lace

FABRICS AND LACE

In the 13th century, Belgium was already famous for woven fabrics and intricate tapestries, made from English wool and exported as far as Asia. By the 16th century, Brussels was renowned for the fine quality of its lace. Lace remains one of the most popular traditional souvenirs of Brussels and Bruges but few Belgian women learn the craft today. As a result, there is not enough handmade lace to meet the demand, and what there is has become very expensive. Many shops now sell lace made in China, which costs less but is inferior. Check out the lace collection at the Musée de Costume et de la Dentelle (➤ 52).

BRUSSELS

LACE GALLERY

Tiny old-fashioned shop specializing in good-quality handmade lace blouses, tablecloths, umbrellas, cushion covers.

➕ E7 ✉ 30 rue du Lombard, corner rue de l'Etuve ☎ 02 513 5830 🕐 Daily 10–7 🚇 Bourse/Beurs 🚊 Tram 23, 52, 55, 56, 81, 90

LACE PALACE

Everything that can possibly be made of lace, both Belgian and imported, old and new. As the name suggests, the Lace Palace is spacious.

➕ E7 ✉ 1–3 rue de la Violette ☎ 02 512 5634 🕐 Daily 8.30–8 🚇 Gare Centrale/Centraal Station

RUBBRECHT

Exquisite old lace pieces, tablecloths and blouses, as well as new Belgian handmade lace. Definitely a cut above the rest.

➕ E7 ✉ 23 Grand' Place ☎ 02 512 0218 🕐 Mon–Sat 9–7; Sun 10–6 🚇 Gare Centrale/Centraal Station

TOEBAC

One of the better lace shops on a street lined with them. Wide selection of blouses, tablecloths, and modern and antique lace, mostly Belgian-made.

➕ E7 ✉ 10 rue Charles Buls ☎ 02 512 0941 🕐 9.30–7 🚊 Tram 23, 52, 55, 56, 81, 90

BRUGES

'T APOSTELIENTJE

This small pretty shop offers professional advice about lacemaking, as well as the tools to make lace, together with ready made old and modern lace to buy.

➕ dIII ✉ Balstraat 11 ☎ 050 33 78 60 🕐 Mon–Sat 9.30–6; Sun 11–4 🚊 6, 16

GRUUTHUSE LACE SHOP

The place to look for fine lace, especially antique pieces. All lace is made in Belgium. Handmade porcelain dolls dressed in antique lace are another feature.

➕ bIII ✉ Dijver 15 ☎ 050 34 30 54 🕐 Summer: daily 10–7. Winter: daily 10–6.30 🚊 1, 6, 11, 16

KANTCENTRUM (LACE CENTRE)

Historical and technical exhibits. Afternoon lacemaking demonstrations, and lacemaking materials on sale. Interesting courses.

➕ dIII ✉ Peperstraat 3a ☎ 050 33 00 72 🕐 Mon–Fri 10–12, 2–6; Sat 10–1, 2–5. 💰 Inexpensive

KANTJUWEELTJE (LACE JEWEL)

Wide selection of handmade new and antique Flemish lace and tapestries. Lacemaking demonstrations take place at 3PM daily.

➕ bIII ✉ Philipstockstraat 11 ☎ 050 33 42 25 🕐 Summer: daily 9–7. Winter: daily 9–6 🚊 4, 8

Crafts, Souvenirs & Gifts

BRUSSELS

AU GRAND RASOIR (MAISON JAMART)

A beautiful specialist knife shop, supplier to the royal family, with an incredible selection for every possible purpose. Repairs, sharpening, re-silvering.

➕ E7 ✉ 7 rue de l'Hôpital (place St.-Jean)
☎ 02 512 4962
🕐 Mon–Sat 9.30–6.30
🚇 Gare Centrale/Centraal Station 🚌 34, 48, 95, 96

LA BOUTIQUE DE TINTIN

Tintin fans come here for everything from pyjamas, socks, cups, and diaries to life-size statues of Tintin and his friend Abdullah and, of course, the books, available in several languages.

➕ E7 ✉ 13 rue de la Colline
☎ 02 514 5152
🕐 Tue–Thu 10–6; Mon 2–6
🚇 Gare Centrale/Centraal Station

THE BRUSSELS CORNER

The souvenirs here are of a better quality and more fun than elsewhere, with a large collection of T-shirts and gift boxes filled with Belgian beers.

➕ E7 ✉ 27 rue de l'Etuve
☎ 02 511 9849
🕐 Daily 9.30–6.30
🚌 34, 48

CHRISTA RENIERS

Beautiful contemporary jewellery with a touch of Zen and no shortage of humour. Reniers' silver cufflinks and keyrings are fun, and the bracelets, rings, and earrings have an elegance all their own.

➕ E7 ✉ 29 rue Antoine Dansaert ☎ 02 514 1773
🕐 Mon–Sat 10.30–6.30
🚌 23; tram 23, 52, 55, 56, 63, 81

SCÈNES DE MÉNAGE

Lovely shop filled with old and modern bed linen and gorgeous pyjamas of the finest quality.

➕ E10 ✉ 4 place Brugmann, Ixelles ☎ 02 344 3295
🕐 Mon–Sat 9.30–6 🚋 Tram 91, 92

BRUGES

BRUGS DIAMANTHUIS

The technique of diamond polishing is attributed to the mid-15th century Bruges goldsmith van Berquem, and Bruges was Europe's first diamond city. This shop keeps alive the tradition of diamond polishing and offers a large selection of quality diamonds and diamond jewellery.

➕ cIII ✉ Katelynestraat 43
☎ 050 33 64 33 🕐 Mon–Fri 10–12, 1.30–5; Sat 10–3
🚌 6, 16

TINTIN SHOP

This shop stocks everything that Tintin fans have ever dreamed of, although there is more choice in the Brussels shop (► this page).

➕ cIII ✉ Steenstraat 3
☎ 050 33 42 92 🕐 Daily 10–6 🚌 All buses

CHALCOGRAPHY

Chalcography is the art of engraving from a copper plate. The Bibliothèque Royale, in Brussels, has an interesting collection of 5,400 engraved plates, including art, flora, and views of Brussels. You can either buy prints over the counter or choose something more unusual from the catalogue, which will then be printed on the traditional presses (✉ Service de Chalcography, in the basement of 1 place du Musée ☎ 02 519 5630 🕐 Mon–Fri 9–12.30, 2–4.45).

Books

STAMPS

Brussels is an important centre for stamp collectors. There are many stamp shops catering for all levels, and most are on or around the rue du Mioli, near the Bourse.

BRUSSELS

BRÜSEL

Large bookshop selling famous comic strips, mainly in French but also in English, Dutch, German, and Spanish.
➕ E7 ✉ 100 boulevard Anspach ☎ 02 502 3552 🕓 Mon–Sat 10.30–6.30 🚇 Bourse/Beurs 🚊 Tram 23, 52, 55, 56, 81

FNAC

Brussel's largest bookshop, with titles in French, Dutch, English, German, Italian, and Spanish, and a good music department.
➕ F6 ✉ City 2, rue Neuve ☎ 02 209 2211 🕓 Mon–Thu, Sat 10–7; Fri 10–8 🚇 Rogier or De Brouckère 🚊 Tram 23, 52, 55, 56, 81

P. GENICOT

Books from the 1600s onwards, mainly French but some in English.
➕ E7 ✉ 6 galerie Bortier on 19 rue St.-Jean ☎ 02 514 1017 🕓 Mon–Sat noon–7 🚇 Gare Centrale/Centraal Station

STERLING

Large English-language bookshop with international magazine and newspaper section, travel books, fiction, and reference books.
➕ E7 ✉ 38 rue du Fossé aux Loups ☎ 02 223 6223 🕓 Mon–Sat 10–7; Sun 12–6.30 🚇 De Brouckère, Gare Centrale/Centraal Station

TROPISMES

Stylish bookshop with books on art, architecture, history, and philosophy, plus English-language titles, coffee-table books, and French literature. Pleasant for browsing.
➕ E7 ✉ galerie des Princes ☎ 02 512 8852; www.tropismes.be 🕓 Mon, Sun 1.30–6.30; Tue–Thu, Sat 10–6.30; Fri 10.30–8 🚇 Gare Centrale/Centraal Station

WATERSTONES

Part of the British chain, with English language books and magazines.
➕ E6 ✉ 71–75 boulevard Adolphe Max ☎ 02 219 2708 🕓 Mon, Wed–Sat 9–6.30; Tue 10–6.30 🚇 Rogier 🚊 Tram 23, 52, 55, 56, 81

BRUGES

RAAKLIJN

Bruges' best bookshop has a good range of foreign-language books, especially paperbacks and art books.
➕ bIII ✉ St.-Jacobsstraat 7 ☎ 050 33 67 20 🕓 Mon–Sat 9–6.30 🚊 All buses

DE REYGHERE

Books in Flemish, French, English, and German, and a wide selection of international newspapers and magazines.
➕ bIII ✉ Markt 12 ☎ 050 33 34 03 🕓 Mon–Thu, Sat 8.30–6.15; Fri 8.30–7 🚊 All buses

DE STRIEP

De Striep specializes in comic strips, mainly Belgian and French, and has a good English section. Also for sale are cartoon characters and collectors' items.
➕ bIII–IV ✉ Katelijnestraat 42 ☎ 050 33 71 12 🕓 Tue–Sat 10–12.30, 1.30–7; Sun 2–6; Mon 1.30–7 🚊 1, 11

Antiques & Secondhand

BRUSSELS

ANTIK BLAES

Two floors of funky, European home and shop furniture (mostly 1940s–1980s), and a few intriguing curiosities.

🚩 E8 📮 51–53 rue Blaes ☎ 02 512 1299 🕐 Daily 10–6 🚌 20, 21, 48

ANTIQUITÉS CLAUDE NOËLLE

Wonderful shop specializing in jewellery from the end of the 19th century to the 1970s.

🚩 E8 📮 20 place du Grand Sablon ☎ 02 511 4172 🕐 Tue–Sat 10.30–6.30; Sun 10.30–2 🚌 All buses

COLLECTOR'S GALLERY

This shop is totally devoted to 20th-century kitsch, such as vintage Barbie dolls, old perfume bottles, cars, and classic toys, all of high quality.

🚩 E8 📮 17 rue Lebeau, Sablon ☎ 02 511 4613 🕐 Tue–Sat 10–6; Sun 10–2 🚌 34, 48, 95, 96; tram 92, 93, 94

GALERIE MODERNE

This huge auction house handles everything from top-of-the-market antiques to junk.

🚩 F8–G8 📮 3 rue du Parnasse ☎ 02 511 5415 🕐 Twice a month. Phone for viewing times 🚇 Trône/Troon 🚌 38, 54, 60, 95, 96

GALERIE VANDERKINDERE

This expensive auction house specializes in art and objects from the 17th and 18th centuries.

🚩 D11–E11 📮 685–687 chaussée d'Alsemberg, St.-Gilles ☎ 02 344 5446 🕐 Mon–Fri 9–12, 2–5. Phone for times of sale 🚌 38; tram 23, 55, 38

GHADIMI

Oriental carpets, *kilims*, and textiles—mainly 19th-century—are stylishly presented in this bright gallery.

🚩 E8 📮 1 rue des Minimes, just off the place du Grand Sablon ☎ 02 512 9841 🕐 Tue–Sun 10–12, 2–6 🚌 34, 48, 95, 96; tram 92, 93, 94

HISTORIC MARINE

Old and antique boat and ship models as well as antique compasses, marine instruments, and paintings of boats. Selected nautical paraphernalia.

🚩 E7 📮 39a rue du Lombard ☎ 02 513 8155 🕐 Mon–Sat 9.30–5.30 🚌 34, 49, 95, 96

BRUGES

THEATER GALERY VAN MULLEM

Small shop hidden on this pretty square with antique Flemish furniture, unusual lights, and wonderful paintings.

🚩 bIII 📮 Vlamingstraat 52 ☎ 050 33 41 41 🕐 Mon–Thu, Sat 10–12, 2–6 🚌 All buses

YANNICK DE HONDT

Stylish antique shop specializing in a weird but successful mixture of 15th–18th century European furniture, antique Japanese furniture, and African art.

🚩 bIII 📮 Mariastraat 12 ☎ 050 34 51 46/0475 65 30 58 🕐 Mon–Sat 2–6 🚌 All buses

---

ANTIQUES IN BRUSSELS

Go to Brussels' Sablon area (► 37) for fine antiques, and to the junk market in Les Marolles (► 38, 60) if you want to browse or bargain hunt. *Brocante*—old collectables—and antique shops on rue Haute and the rue Blaes are good for furniture but becoming fashionable, so the prices aren't the bargains they once were. Check out the streets behind the church on place du Jeu de Balles.

Food

BELGIAN COOKIES

Pain à lo Grecque is a light crispy cookie covered in tiny bits of sugar, while *speculoos* is a finer version of gingerbread. The *coucque de Dinant* is a hard, bread-like cookie that comes in beautiful shapes—windmills, rabbits, peasants, cars, and more. *Peperkoek* is a spicy cake laced with sugar or almonds.

BRUSSELS

AU SUISSE

The traditional deli to buy smoked fish, cheeses, *charcuterie* (cold cuts), and other delicacies. Try the house special dish, *filet Américain*, a steak tartare. The sandwich bar next door of the same name is also a Brussels institution.

➕ E7 ✉ 73–75 boulevard Anspach ☎ 02 512 9589 🕐 Mon–Fri 10–8; Sat, Sun 10–9 Ⓜ Bourse/Beurs 🚊 Tram 23, 52, 55, 56, 81

DANDOY

A beautiful bakery, founded in 1829, selling traditional Brussels cookies such as *pain à la Grecque*, *speculoos*, and *coucque de Dinant* in all sizes and shapes, as well as Belgium's best marzipan. Once you are inside, this place is hard to resist!

➕ E7 ✉ 31 rue au Beurre (other branch at 14 rue Charles Buls) ☎ 02 513 1057 🕐 Mon–Sat 8.30–6.30; Sun 10–6.30 Ⓜ Bourse/Beurs 🚊 Tram 23, 52, 55, 56, 81

FROMAGERIE MAISON BAGUETTE–GASPARD

A master cheese-seller with an amazing array of cheeses, particularly French and Belgian, many made by monks in Belgian abbeys.

➕ F8 ✉ 28 rue de la Longue Vie, Ixelles ☎ 02 511 7095 Ⓜ Porte de Namur 🚊 34, 80

LE PAIN QUOTIDIEN/ HET DAGELIJKS BROOD (➤ 66)

PATISSERIE WITTAMER

This wonderful but expensive patisserie sells the best sorbets in town, excellent handmade chocolates, and cakes that taste as good as they look.

➕ E8 ✉ 12–13 place du Grand Sablon ☎ 02 512 3742 🕐 Mon 8–6; Tue–Sat 7–7; Sun 7–6 🚊 34, 48, 95, 96; tram 92, 93, 94;

BRUGES

DIKSMUIDS BOTERHUIS

A wonderful shop with hams and sausages hanging from the ceiling, and a good choice of Belgian and French cheeses and breads. Service can be slow but it's worth the wait.

➕ bIII ✉ 23 Geldmuntstraat ☎ No phone 🕐 Tue–Sun 10–12, 2–6 🚊 All buses

MALESHERBES

Small shop specializing in good French wines, artisanal foie gras from Périgord in France, homemade terrines, and farmhouse cheeses. Next door is a small bistro.

➕ bIV ✉ 8 Stoofstraat ☎ 0477 74 14 13 🕐 Wed–Sun 12–1.45, 7–9.30 🚊 1

TEMMERMAN

Good old-fashioned candies, sugared almonds, *speculoos*, and fine handmade chocolates in the shape of sea creatures or pebbles, all stored in large jars.

➕ bIII ✉ Zilverpand, Noordzandstraat 63 ☎ 050 33 16 78 🕐 Mon 2–6.30; Tue–Thu 10–12.30, 2–6.30; Fri, Sat 10–6.30 🚊 All buses

Belgian Chocolates

BRUSSELS

GALLER

Delicious pralines and chocolate bars in many flavours. Belgian Royal Warrant Holder.

➕ E7 ✉ 44 rue au Beurre
☎ 02 502 0266 🕐 Daily
10–9.30 🚇 Bourse/Beurs
🚋 Tram 23, 52, 55, 56, 81

GODIVA

The most famous *chocolatier* of all, with shops around the world.

➕ E7 ✉ 22 Grand' Place
☎ 02 511 2537 🕐 Mon–Sat
9AM–midnight; Sun 10AM–midnight 🚇 Gare Centrale/Centraal Station

MARY'S

This old-fashioned shop, specializing in homemade pralines and wonderful *marrons glacés*, is well known among Brussels' chocolate lovers.

➕ F6–F7 ✉ 73 rue Royale
☎ 02 217 4500 🕐 Tue–Fri,
Sat 2–5 🚇 Botanique/Kruidtuin 🚋 Tram 92, 93, 94

PIERRE MARCOLINI

Marcolini is winner of the Chocolatier of the World award, and his often-sculpted chocolate creations, with high cocoa content, are some of the best, and most expensive, in Belgium. (Also at 75 avenue Louise and 1302 chaussée de Waterloo).

➕ E8 ✉ place du Grand
Sablon ☎ 02 514 1206
🕐 Tue–Sun 10–6 🚋 34, 48,
95, 96; tram 92, 93, 94

PLANÈTE CHOCOLAT

"Chocolate is art" is Frank Duval's slogan. You can watch him make and sculpt wonderful artworks or pralines on the premises. If you're a serious chocoholic don't miss the tea room, with its chocolates, cakes, and ice creams.

➕ E7 ✉ 24 rue du Lombard
☎ 02 511 0755 🕐 Daily
9–6.30; on fine, summer days until 10PM 🚇 Bourse/Beurs
🚋 Tram 23, 52, 55, 56, 81

WITTAMER (▶ 76)

BRUGES

DEPLA

Delicious handmade chocolates. Special treats include truffles, florentines, chocolates with nuts and raisins, and good marzipan wrapped in chocolate. There is a branch at Eekhoutstraat 23.

➕ blll ✉ Huidenvettersplein
13 ☎ 050 34 74 12 🕐 Daily
10–6.30 🚌 6, 16

SPEGHELAERE

Bruges' best kept secret, this *chocolatier* is a far cry from the many chocolate shops catering for tourists. All chocolates are made on the premises, and the house special is a bunch of grapes made from marzipan covered in black chocolate. A paradise for chocoholics.

➕ bll ✉ Ezelstraat 92
☎ 050 33 60 52 🕐 Tue–Sat
8.15–12.15, 1.15–7; Sun 9–1
🚌 3, 13

SWEERTVAEGHER

Luxurious handmade pralines.

➕ blll ✉ Philipstockstraat 29
☎ 050 33 83 67 🕐 Tue–Sat
9.30–6.30 🚌 6, 16

CHOCOLATE CHAINS

The Swiss claim that they produce the best chocolate in the world but this is hotly disputed in Belgium. The Swiss may market it more effectively, but Belgian chocolate is as good, if not better. The Leonidas chain, less expensive than the shops mentioned here, sells very good quality chocolates, and the beautifully wrapped Côte d'Or bars are worth seeking out in supermarkets.

Belgian Fashion

BRUSSELS SHOPPING STREETS

Avenue Louise (➤ 39) is the traditional shopping area, with everything from Chanel to the Belgian designer Olivier Strelli. The fashionable place to shop, however, is rue Antoine Dansaert, which has the best shoe shops in Brussels and several shops of new designers. Most Belgian designers, including Walter Van Bierendonk, Ann Demeulemeester, Dries Van Noten, Dirk Bikkembeug, Veronique Branquiinho, and Chris Mestdagh (the Belgian Paul Smith), have flagship stores in Antwerp, but are available at the Stijl, the large store that is the grand temple of Belgian fashion. All these designers produce accessible avant-garde fashion, while designers such as Chine and Olivier Strelli produce more commercial clothes, and Kaat Tilley stands out for her amazingly textured clothes. Apart from the several Stijl shops, other shops and new designers have opened their doors on Dansaert, including Annemie Verbeke.

BRUSSELS

CHINE
This Belgian designer offers Hong Kong designs, mainly silk, wool, and cotton, dyed in beautiful colours.
➕ E7 ✉ 2 rue Van Antevelde ☎ 02 503 1449 ⏰ Mon–Sat 10–6.30 🚇 Bourse/Beurs 🚋 Tram 23, 52, 55, 56, 81

ELVIS POMPILLO
This Liège-born hatmaker, who really *is* called Elvis Pompillo, makes some very wearable and some outrageous hats for men, women, and kids—always with a quirky twist.
➕ E7 ✉ 10 rue du Midi ☎ 02 511 1188 ⏰ Mon–Sat 10.30–6.30 🚋 34, 38; tram 23, 52, 55, 56, 81

KAAT TILLEY
Tilley's loose, sculptured clothes for women in luscious fabrics defy description, while the shop belongs in a fairy tale. Her clothes are hugely popular in Japan and in New York, where she has opened two more shops.
➕ E7 ✉ 4 Galerie du Roi ☎ 02 514 0763 ⏰ Mon–Fri 10–6; Sat 10.30–6.30 🚇 Gare Centrale/Centraal Station 🚋 29, 63, 66, 71

OLIVIER STRELLI
Streamlined, modern fashion for men and women in blacks, beiges, greys, and browns, with an occasional dash of colour.
➕ F9 ✉ 72 avenue Louise ☎ 02 512 5607 ⏰ Mon–Sat 10–6 🚇 Louise 🚋 Tram 93, 94

STIJL
This fashion giant sells the collections of established designers such as Dries Van Noten, Bikkembergs, as well as the newcomers, in bare and cold industrial surroundings. You'll find men's and women's clothes here, and sister shops down the street selling trendy children's clothes (Kat en Muis) and beautiful lingerie (Stijl Underwear, 47 rue Antoine Dansaert).
➕ E7 ✉ 74 rue Antoine Dansaert ☎ 02 512 0313 ⏰ Mon–Sat 10.30–6.30 🚇 Bourse/Beurs 🚋 63; tram 23, 52, 55, 56, 81

BRUGES

L'HEROÏNE
The only shop in Bruges with a wide selection of Belgian fashion designers, including Kaat Tilley, Chris Janssens, and Dries Van Noten. Also fashion accessories and Belgian jewellery.
➕ bIII ✉ Noordzandstraat 32 ☎ 050 33 56 57 ⏰ Mon–Sat 10–6.30 🚋 All buses

OLIVIER STRELLI
A branch of the Brussels' fashion store.
➕ bIII ✉ Eiermarkt 3 ☎ 050 34 38 37 ⏰ Mon–Sat 10–6 🚋 All buses

Offbeat & Unusual

BRUSSELS

AZZATO

Musical instruments, including ethnic instruments and drums.

✚ E7 ✉ 42 rue de la Violette ☎ 02 512 37 52 🕐 Mon–Sat 9.30–6 🚋 Bourse/Beurs 🚋 Tram 23, 52, 55, 56, 81

LA COURTE ECHELLE

This tiny shop specializes in dolls houses and also organizes workshops.

✚ E7 ✉ 12 rue des Eperonniers ☎ 02 512 4759 🕐 Mon, Tue, Thu–Sat 11.30–1.30, 2–6 🚇 Gare Centrale/Centraal Station

IDIZ BOGAM

Fashionable selection of secondhand clothes and shoes. A branch is at 76 rue Antoine Dansaert.

✚ E8 ☎ 162 rue Blaes ☎ 02 502 8337 🕐 Daily 10.30–6 🚋 20, 48 🚇 Porte de Hal/Hallepoort

PICARD

Europe's largest party store is a wonderful place. Fancy dresses for sale or rent, masks, party tricks, and magicians' equipment.

✚ E7 ✉ 71–75 rue du Lombard ☎ 02 513 0790 🕐 Mon–Sat 9–6 🚋 34, 48

ROYAL DOG SHOP

"Le Couturier pour Chiens" says it all. Diamond collars, cardigans, raincoats, and accessories for Fido, made to measure or ready-made.

✚ E7 ✉ 27–28 place de la Justice/Justitieplein ☎ 02 513 3261 🕐 Mon, Wed–Sat 9–6 🚋 34, 48

SERNEELS

A spacious shop with a wonderful (but expensive) selection of toys, from tiny ducklings to full-size cars, camels, and beautiful rocking horses.

✚ F9 ✉ 69 avenue Louise ☎ 02 538 3066 🕐 Mon–Sat 9.30–6.30 🚋 Tram 93, 94

BRUGES

BAZAR BIZAR

Decorative objects, gifts, and jewellery imported from all over the world.

✚ bIII ✉ St.-Jakobstraat 3/5 ☎ 050 33 80 16 🕐 Mon–Sat 10–12.30, 2–6.30 🚌 All buses

HOET OPTIEK

Funky optician with spectacles "to be seen in."

✚ b–dIII ✉ Vlamingstraat 19 ☎ 050 33 50 02 🕐 Mon–Fri 9.30–6 🚌 All buses

OUD TEGELHUIS

Amusing shop stocking bygone tins and posters.

✚ cIII ✉ Peerdenstraat 2 ☎ 050 34 01 03 🕐 Wed–Sun 2–6 🚌 1, 6, 11, 16

ROMBAUX

Lovely old-fashioned store with sheet music, CDs, and instruments.

✚ cIII ✉ Mallebergstraat 13 ☎ 050 33 25 75 🕐 Mon–Sat 9–12.30, 2–6.30 🚌 All buses to the Markt

DE WITTE PELIKAAN

Christmas wrappings and tree decorations from around the world.

✚ bIII ✉ Vlamingstraat 23 ☎ 050 34 82 84 🕐 Mon–Sat 11–6 🚌 All buses

OLD-FASHIONED TOYS

The In den Olifant chain sells beautifully made wooden toys, mobiles, puppets, and musical instruments. Pricey but worth it.

✉ 47 rue des Fripiers, Brusssels ☎ 02 217 4397; ✉ St.-Jacobsstraat 47, Bruges ☎ 050 32 75 79

Jazz, Pop & Nightlife

NIGHTSPOTS

From elegant art nouveau cafés and smoky old joints full of local pensioners to the crowded bars of rue du Marché au Charbon, you'll find it all within walking distance of the Grand' Place. As there are so many good bars to meet their friends, Belgians socialize a great deal. Most Brussels clubs open at 11PM but don't start to fill before midnight–don't start out too early. The English and Australians, used to drinking up before the pubs close at 11PM, may need some stamina. It is customary to buy rounds for your friends or for whoever paid the last one.

BRUSSELS

L'ACROBAT (➤ 70)

ANCIENNE BELGIQUE
One of Brussels' best rock venues, revamped as a showcase for the Flemish community, has concerts by major artists. A club above hosts other gigs.
✚ E7 ✉ 114 boulevard Anspach ☎ 02 548 2424 Ⓠ Bourse/Beurs 🚊 Tram 23, 52, 55, 56, 81

L'ARCHIDUC (➤ 70)

BEURSSCHOUWBURG
The 19th-century theatre of the Stock Exchange is now a venue for rock concerts, jazz, North African *rai*, and avant-garde Belgian theatre.
✚ E7 ✉ 22 rue Auguste Orts ☎ 02 513 8290 Ⓠ Bourse/Beurs 🚊 34, 47, 48, 63, 95, 96; tram 23, 52, 55, 56, 81

LE BOTANIQUE
The botanical gardens were turned into a cultural centre for the French-speaking community. There are rock concerts in the Orangerie and world music events such as the Festival de la Chanson, during September.
✚ F6 ✉ 236 rue Royale ☎ 02 226 1211 Ⓠ Botanique 🚊 38, 61; tram 92, 94

CARNOA QUEBRADA
One of several Latin American clubs in this area. Strong, smooth *caipirinhas* cocktails make it easy to salsa.
✚ E7 ✉ 53 rue du Marché au Charbon ☎ 02 511 1354 ◉ Thu–Sat 10–dawn 🚊 Tram 23, 52, 55, 56, 81

CIRQUE ROYAL
Great circular hall in a former circus, with usherettes to show you to your seat. Good gigs.
✚ F7 ✉ 81 rue de l'Enseignement ☎ 02 218 2015 Ⓠ Madou 🚊 63

LE FOOL MOON
Dance-based acts, soul, and acid-jazz. Excellent DJs.
✚ C7–D7 ✉ 126 quai de Mariemont ☎ 02 410 1003 ◉ Sat only Ⓠ Gare l'Ouest/Weststation 🚊 63; tram 18

FOREST NATIONAL
One of Belgium's largest venues draws many major bands and stars, despite the bad acoustics and endless parking problems.
✚ C11 ✉ 36 avenue du Globe ☎ 0900 00991 ◉ All year round, times vary 🚊 48, 54; tram 18, 52

THE FUSE
Brussels' first techno club maintains excellent standards, with DJs from London, the US, and Amsterdam. The place is drab, but the crowds don't notice.
✚ E8 ✉ 208 rue Blaes ☎ 02 511 9789 ◉ Sat 11PM–7AM Ⓠ Porte de Hal 🚊 20, 48

MAGASIN 4
This former warehouse is where many up-and-coming rock bands perform for the first time in the country. It's a great place to watch new Flemish bands as well.
✚ E6 ✉ 4 rue du Magasin ☎ 02 223 3474 ◉ Check listings Ⓠ Yser/Ijzer 🚊 Tram 18

MIRANO CONTINENTAL

Fashionable crowds of thirtysomethings frequent this former cinema where house music is king.

🞧 G7 ✉ 38 chaussée de Louvain ☎ 02 218 5772
🕐 Sat 11PM–late
🚇 Madou
🚌 29, 63

NEW YORK CAFÉ JAZZ CLUB

Smart, brasserie-type restaurant with jazz venue behind featuring local acts. Popular with celebrities.

🞧 F8 ✉ place Stéphanie
☎ 02 534 8509
🕐 Fri–Sat 10PM–late
🚇 Louise/Louiza
🚌 91, 92, 93, 94

SOUNDS

Great jazz café that regularly features the best international and local jazz musicians. Near the place Ferdinand Lecocq, which is well-stocked with good bars.

🞧 F8 ✉ rue de la Tulipe 28, Ixelles ☎ 02 512 9250
🕐 Mon–Sat noon–4AM
🚇 Porte de Namur/Naamse Poort

VK

This is the best alternative venue in town, regularly featuring hiphop, punk, ragga, rock, and indie bands.

🞧 D6 ✉ rue de l'Ecole, Molenbeek ☎ 02 414 2907
🕐 Times vary
🚇 Comte de Flandre/Graaf van Vlaanderen (this area is known for street crime, so when you leave the club at night take a taxi to the Bourse, rather than taking the metro from Comte de Flandre)

WHO'S WHO LAND

Vast and very popular super-trendy house club. If you love wearing latex outfits and occasionally rolling in foam, then this is the place to be.

🞧 E8–7 ✉ 17 rue de Poinçon, Marolles ☎ 02 512 5270 🕐 Fri, Sat 11PM–4AM
🚇 Anneesens

BRUGES

DE CACTUS CLUB

The main venue in town for rock, jazz, and world music. The club also organizes an open-air festival in Minnewater Park during the second weekend of July. A music café at No. 36 on the same street is hugely popular with locals.

🞧 blll ✉ St.-Jacobsstraat 33
☎ 050 33 20 14 🚌 3, 13

L'aMARAL

Trendy and hugely popular disco.

🞧 clll ✉ Kuipersstraat 10
☎ No phone 🕐 Thu, Fri, Sat 10PM–4AM, and often on other days 🚌 All buses

DE VERSTEENDE NACHT

Intimate, smoky café run by a jazz aficionado. Free jazz concerts and jam sessions every Wednesday.

🞧 clll ✉ Langestraat 11
☎ 050 34 32 93 🕐 Tue–Thu 7PM–2AM; Fri 7PM–4AM

VILLA ROMANA

Popular mock Roman club especially crowded on weekends.

🞧 blll ✉ Kraanplein 1
☎ 050 34 34 53 🕐 Daily 10PM–late 🚌 3, 4, 6, 8, 13, 16

GAY BRUSSELS

The two lesbian bars are Pussy Galore (✉ 208 rue Blaes 🕐 2nd Fri of month) and Sappho (✉ 1 rue St.-Géry 🕐 Fri, Sat 10PM–late). There are bars for gay men around rue des Pierres, in addition to Le Belgica (✉ 32 rue du Marché au Charbon), Tels Quels (✉ 81 rue du Marché au Charbon), and La Démence (✉ 208 rue Blaes).

GAY BRUGES

The Bruges gay scene, located on the outskirts of the city, is low key. Boomerang is the gay centre with Café del Mar for gays and lesbians (✉ Spoorwegstraart, St.-Michiels). Ravel is also a gay bar (✉ Karel de Stoutelaan 172 ☎ 02 31 52 74).

Opera & Classical Music

TICKETS

Tickets for most big events in Brussels can be booked (at a small charge) through the Tourist Office on the Grand' Place (☎ 02 513 8940); Auditorium 44 (☎ 02 218 2735) on boulevard du Jardin Botanique 44; or FNAC in City2, rue Neuve (☎ 02 209 2239).

BRUSSELS

CHAPELLE ROYALE

Beautiful small hall with perfect acoustics, a favourite with chamber orchestras. Book early.
✚ F7–F8 ✉ 5 Coudenberg ☎ 02 673 0581 🚇 Gare Centrale/Centraal Station

CONSERVATOIRE ROYAL DE MUSIQUE

Another perfect venue for chamber orchestras, partly designed by the famous organ builder Cavaillé-Coll.
✚ F7 ✉ 30 rue de la Régence ☎ 02 511 0427, in the Palais de Beaux Arts 🚇 Gare Centrale/Centraal Station or Louise

ÉGLISE DES ST.-JEAN ET ST.-ETIENNE AUX MINIMES

Many concerts are held in this high-baroque church near Les Marolles. The Philharmonic Society has early-music recitals, and on Sundays the La Chapelle des Minimes ensemble performs Bach cantatas. Admission fees are voluntary.
✚ E8 ✉ 62 rue des Minimes ☎ 02 507 8200 🕒 Lunchtime throughout the summer. One Sun a month at 10.30AM 🚌 48

PALAIS DES BEAUX ARTS

This art nouveau complex is Brussels' most prestigious concert venue. Its two halls, with perfect acoustics, are home to the acclaimed Philharmonic Society and the Orchestre National de Belgique. Most of the city's big concerts take place here.
✚ F7 ✉ 23 rue Ravenstein ☎ Box office: 02 507 8200; 24-hour information 02 507 8444; www.pbapsk.be 🕒 Box office: Mon–Sat 9–7 🚇 Parc/Park or Gare Centrale/Centraal Station

THÉÂTRE DE LA MONNAIE

The national opera house is Brussels' pride. Since a sumptuous renovation in the 1980s, innovation and excellence have been hallmarks, first under Gerard Mortier and now under director Bernard Foccroulle, himself a musician. Performances sell out well in advance. (▶ 57).
✚ E7 ✉ place de la Monnaie ☎ 02 229 1211 🕒 Box office Tue–Sat 11–5.30 🚇 De Brouckère

BRUGES

Bruges hosts several classical music festivals a year, including the Flanders Festival, which takes place in churches all over the city in summer. For information check with the tourist office.

CONCERTGEBOUW

Opened in 2002, the Concertgebouw aims to attract the best of international and national performers in its large and perfectly equipped performance halls (▶ 57).
✚ bIII ✉ t'Zandt ☎ 050 47 69 99; www.concertgebouw.be 🚌 1–9, 11, 13, 15–17, 25

STADSSCHOUWBURG

Renovated performance hall for theatre and music.
✚ b–cIII ✉ Vlamingstraat 29 ☎ 050 44 30 60 🚌 3, 4, 8

Theatre & Dance

BRUSSELS

CIRQUE ROYAL (► 80)
The best dance theatre, showing mostly contemporary dance.

KAAITHEATER
A jewel of 1930s architecture, this former cinema houses the Flemish Theatre Institute. There are occasional performances in English, and also performances by influential Belgian dancers such as Anne Teresa De Keersmaeker, Jan Fabre, and Discordia.
🞦 D6 ✉ 20 square Sainctelette ☎ Box office 02 201 5959 🚇 Yser/IJzer

PALAIS DES BEAUX ARTS (► 82)

THÉÂTRE 140
This venue is rather scruffy but offers excellent performances, both dance and theatre, by the best touring troupes.
🞦 H6 ✉ 140 avenue Eugène Plasky ☎ 02 733 9708 🚇 Box office: Mon–Sat 11–6 🚌 29, 63; tram 23, 90

THÉÂTRE NATIONAL
The National Theatre often arranges co-productions with Strasbourg. Most plays are in French, with the occasional English-speaking touring company.
🞦 F6 ✉ Centre Rogier, place Rogier ☎ 02 203 5303 🚇 Box office Mon–Sat 11–6 🚇 Rogier

THÉÂTRE ROYAL DU PARC
Stunning theatre with excellent French productions as well as old-fashioned and now unique 1930s *pièces de boulevard* (experimental theatre that was originally performed in the street).
🞦 F7 ✉ 3 rue de la Loi ☎ 02 512 2339 🚇 Box Office daily 11–6 🚇 Arts–Loi/Kunst–Wet or Parc/Park

THÉÂTRE DE TOONE
Adorable little marionette theatre, famous for productions of classics such as *Hamlet* and *Faust* performed in Bruxellois, the Brussels dialect, a strange mixture of French and Flemish. The café is fun and open all day.
🞦 E7 ✉ 6 impasse Schuddeveld, petite rue des Bouchers ☎ 02 511 7137 🚇 Tue–Sat noon–midnight 🚇 Gare Centrale/Centraal Station

BRUGES

CONCERTGEBOUW (► 57, 82)

CULTUURCENTRUM
Four venues under one name, including the Stadsschouwburg, the city's theatre, with performances mostly in Flemish.
🞦 bIII ✉ St.-Jacobsstraat 20–26 ☎ 050 44 30 40. Box office: 050 44 30 60 🚇 Box office: Mon–Fri 10–1, 2–6; Sat 10–1 🚇 All buses

BELGIUM DANCES

Belgium's reputation for contemporary dance has flourished since Frenchman Maurice Béjart founded his Twentieth Century Dance Company and the Mudra school in 1953–and revolutionized dance in the country. There are now more than 50 companies in residence in Brussels, most of them very contemporary. The new choreographers Anne Teresa De Keersmaeker and Wim Vandekeybus are already famous around the world.

Cinemas

SUBTITLES AND DUBBING

Foreign films in Bruges' cinemas are always subtitled; in Brussels you may find a dubbed version. If that matters, be alert in the listings in daily newspapers or the English-language *Bulletin* for the following abbreviations: *VO* means *version originale*, subtitled; *V fr*, French version; *V angl*, English version; *EA* means *enfants admis*, children admitted; *ENA* means children under 16 are not admitted.

BRUSSELS

ACTORS STUDIO

Small two-screen repertory cinema presenting five films a day, mainly "B" movies and good films from non-European countries.
➕ E7 ✉ 16 petite rue des Bouchers ☎ 02 512 1696 🚇 Gare Centrale/Centraal Station

ARENBERG GALERIES

This tiny but delightful cinema in a converted art deco theatre in the Galeries St.-Hubert specializes in repertory cinema and foreign films. It's an excellent place to see some of the better films coming out of Asia and the Middle East.
➕ E7 ✉ 26 galerie de la Reine ☎ 02 512 8063 🚇 Gare Centrale/Centraal Station

KINEPOLIS

Vast cinema complex in the Bruparck with 25 screens and the largest IMAX screen in Europe (it seats 7,000). Mainstream movies, mainly Hollywood stuff.
➕ D2 ✉ Bruparck (➤ 58), 1 avenue du Cinquantenaire ☎ Bookings: 02 474 2604. French information: 0900 35 241. Flemish information: 0900 35 240 🚇 Heysel/Heizel

MUSÉE DU CINÉMA

Besides the permanent exhibition, five films are shown daily, two of which are silent films accompanied by piano music. This is the place to see the old cinema classics, as well as more recent movies and little-known jewels from Third World countries.
➕ F7 ✉ 9 rue Baron Horta ☎ 02 507 8370 🕐 Daily 5.30–10.30 🚇 Gare Centrale/Centraal Station 🚌 20, 29, 38, 60, 63, 65, 66, 71, 95, 96; tram 92, 93, 94

STYX

A small repertory cinema with films in the original language, often English.
➕ F8 ✉ rue de l'Arbre Bénit 72, Ixelles ☎ 02 512 2102 🚇 Porte de Namur

UGC DE BROUCKÈRE

Ten well-equipped auditoriums, including the 70mm UCG Gran Eldorado. Mainly Hollywood productions.
➕ E7 ✉ 38 place De Brouckère ☎ 0900 10 440 (French); 0900 10 450 (Flemish) 🚇 De Brouckère

BRUGES

KENNEDY

The two cinemas here screen mainstream movies as well as art films on certain evenings.
➕ bIII ✉ Zilverstraat 14 ☎ 050 33 20 70 🕐 See newspapers or display at the tourist office 🚌 All buses

LIBERTY

Mainstream films in the subtitled original version.
➕ bIII ✉ Kuipersstraat 23 ☎ 050 33 20 11 🚌 All buses

LUMIÈRE

The Theatre De Korre's two screens feature mainly foreign "B" films and better Belgian productions.
➕ bIII ✉ St.-Jacobsstraat 36A ☎ 050 33 48 57 🚌 All buses

Sports

CYCLING

Not surprisingly in such a flat country, cycling is big in Belgium. Most races are in the countryside. The Grand Prix Eddy Merckx, named after one of the greatest Belgian cyclists, draws speed cyclists to Brussels in May–June. The Forêt de Soignes (► 59) in Brussels has pleasant, very good cycling paths, and the ride from Bruges to Damme or to Knokke (► 21) has several splendid views. To rent a bicycle, you could try Pro Vélo, in Brussels (☎ 02 502 7355), which also organizes cycle tours. At most railway stations you can purchase a train-plus-vélo ticket, which combines bicycle rental with train travel (☎ 02 555 2525).
For more information on bicycling ► 91.

GOLF

There are over 60 golf courses in Belgium; information from the Fédération Royal Belge de Golf (☎ 02 672 2389).

JOGGING

In Brussels, people jog in parc du Cinquantenaire (► 32), parc de Bruxelles (► 36), or parc de Woluwe (✉ avenue de Tervuren 🚊 Tram 39, 44). In Bruges, they jog in the parks around the city (► 41) or in Tillegembos woods, St.-Michiels (☎ 050 38 02 96 🚊 25). The Brussels Half Marathon, held on the last Sunday in May, attracts 20,000 competitors (Bruxelles Promotion 1886 ☎ 02 511 9000). The Ivo Van Damme Memorial, one of Brussels' most important athletic events, is in August. The Brussels Marathon is in September. Information from the tourist office (☎ 02 513 8940).

ROLLER SKATING

Patinoire Du Heysal (Brussels Roller Club)is at: ✉ 134 avenue de Madiudlaen ☎ 02 345 1611 🚇 Heysel/Heizel.
In-line skaters and skateboarders gather behind the Gare Centrale on the Monts des Arts, or in the Bois de le Cambre on Sundays when the roads are closed.

SOCCER

Bruges has two teams in the Belgian first division, Club Brugge and Cercle Brugge. Brussels-based RSC Anderlecht is Belgium's favourite team. It is often in European competitions and is arch rival of Club Brugge.
RSC Anderlecht ✉ Vanden Stock Stadium, 2 avenue Theo Verbeeck ☎ 02 522 1539 🚇 St.-Guidon/St.-Guido;
Club Brugge ✉ Jan Breydel Stadium, Olympialaan ☎ 050 40 21 21 🚊 25;
Cercle Brugge ✉ Jan Breydel Stadium, Olympialaan ☎ 050 38 91 93 🚊 25

WALKING

The best place for a long walk near Brussels' centre is the Fôret de Soignes (► 59). Maps are available from the tourist office. In Bruges, you can walk in Tillegembos (► this page) or along the canal to Damme (► 21).

RACING AT THE HIPPODROME

Horse racing is becoming increasingly popular and there are several racetracks around Brussels. Events often feature chariot-style racing rather than races with the more conventional mounted jockeys.
Hippodrome de Boitsfort:
✉ 51 chausée de la Hulpe
☎ 02 660 2839
🚊 41; tram 94
Hippodrome de Groenendael:
✉ 54 St.-Jansbergen, Hoeilaart
☎ 02 657 3820
🚊 366
Hippodrome de Sterrebeek:
✉ 43 avenue du Roy de Blicquylaan
☎ 02 767 5475
🚊 30; tram 39

Hotels

PRICES

Expect to pay the following for a double room with breakfast
€   less than €100
€€   €100–€200
€€€   more than €200

INEXPENSIVE HOTELS

Many hotels in Brussels are business-orientated, so in summer and at weekends prices can drop by up to 50 percent. The Belgian Tourist Reservations office on Grand' Place (☎ 02 513 7484; fax 02 513 9277) has a free list of over 800 hotels offering off-peak reductions. Although this makes it difficult to reserve far in advance, hotels are rarely full in these periods. Bed-and-breakfast accommodation can be arranged in Brussels (☎ 02 646 0737; fax 02 644 0144; www.bnb-brussels.be).

BRUSSELS

AGENDA LOUISE (€€)

Friendly service and 38 comfortable rooms, close to avenue Louise. Book well ahead.
✚ F9 ✉ 6 rue de Florence, Ixelles ☎ 02 539 0031; fax 02 539 0063; www.hotel-agenda.com 🚇 Louise/Louiza 🚋 Tram 91

ALFA SABLON (€€–€€€)

Modern, efficient 32-room hotel with all amenities but no character in an area full of antique shops.
✚ E8 ✉ 2–8 rue de la Paille, Sablon ☎ 02 513 6040; fax 02 511 8141; www.alfahotels.com 🚋 Tram 91, 92, 93, 94

AMIGO (€€€)

One of Brussels' finest hotels, in the style of an 18th-century mansion. Friendly staff and 176 elegantly furnished rooms. A favourite with ministers and French media stars.
✚ E7 ✉ 1–3 rue de l'Amigo, central ☎ 02 547 4747; fax 02 513 5277; www.hotelamigo.com 🚇 Bourse/Beurs, Gare Centrale 🚌 34, 48, 94

ASTORIA (€€€)

This hotel near the Royal Palace was built in the 19th century for royal visitors. It's full of stories: The Aga Khan liked his bath filled with milk and artist Salvador Dalí gave wild press conferences here. The palm trees and chandeliers are still there, but modern facilities have been added. 118 rooms.
✚ F7 ✉ 103 rue Royale, central ☎ 02 227 0505; fax 02 217 1150; www.sofitel.com 🚇 Gare Centrale/Centraal Station

LA BOURSE (€)

Budget hotel in the trendy St.-Géry district. The rooms are nothing special, but they are clean and the reception is friendly.
✚ E7 ✉ 11 rue Antoine Dansaert, central ☎ 02 512 6010; fax 02 512 6139 🚇 Bourse/Beurs

COMFORT ART HOTEL SIRU (€€)

Each of the 101 rooms in this 1930s hotel has work by a different Belgian artist. The higher you go, the better the views.
✚ F6 ✉ 1 place Rogier, central ☎ 02 203 3580; fax 02 203 3303; www.comforthotel siru.com 🚇 Rogier

CONRAD INTERNATIONAL (€€€)

One of Brussels' finest modern hotels. The lobby, with marble floors and chandeliers, is a prelude to the 269 luxurious rooms.
✚ F9 ✉ 72 avenue Louise, Ixelles ☎ 02 542 4242; fax 02 542 4200; www.brussels.conrad international.com 🚋 Tram 93, 94

LE DIXSEPTIÈME (€€€)

Stylish hotel in the 17th-century former residence of the Spanish ambassador. 24 elegant rooms around a tranquil courtyard.
✚ E7 ✉ 25 rue de la Madeleine ☎ 02 502 5744; fax 02 502 6424; www.ledixseptieme.be 🚇 Gare Centrale/Centraal Station

LA LÉGENDE (€)

Attractive 26-room courtyard hotel.
✚ E7 ✉ 35 rue du Lombard, central ☎ 02 512 8290; fax 02 512 3493; www.hotellalegende. com 🚋 Tram 23, 52, 55, 56, 81

MELIA AVENUE LOUISE (€€–€€€)

An 80-room boutique hotel, near the city's major shopping area and within walking distance of the main sights. The decor is sumptuous and traditional. ✚ F9 ✉ 4 rue Blanche, Ixelles ☎ 02 535 9500; fax 02 535 9600; www.solmelia.com Ⓜ Louise

METROPOLE (€€€)

Belgium's grandest hotel (410 rooms) is a Brussels institution, built in 1895. Popular with media stars. ✚ E6 ✉ 31 place De Brouckère, central ☎ 02 217 2300; fax 02 218 0220; www.metropolehotel.com Ⓜ De Brouckère 🚊 Tram 23, 52, 55, 56, 81

ST.-MICHEL (€€)

Family-run, 15-room hotel behind the grand gilded facade of the House of the Duke of Brabant. The furniture is worth putting up with when you wake up with a view over one of Europe's most beautiful squares. Remember, though, that revellers on the Grand' Place can be rather noisy. ✚ E7 ✉ 15 Grand' Place, central ☎ 02 511 0956; fax 02 511 4600 Ⓜ Gare Centrale/Centraal Station 🚊 Tram 23, 52, 55, 56, 81

SLEEP WELL (€)

This former YMCA offers comfortable rooms at hostel rates. ✚ F6 ✉ 23 rue du Damier, Central ☎ 02 218 5050; fax 02 218 1313; www.sleepwell.be Ⓜ Rogier or Botanique 🚊 Tram 91, 92, 93, 94

BRUGES

BAUHAUS (€)

Popular central hostal with free sheets and showers. ✚ clll ✉ Langestraat 135 ☎ 050 34 10 93; fax 050 33 41 80; www.bauhaus.be 🚌 6, 16

BED & BREAKFAST MARIE-PAULE GESQUIÈRE (€)

Three comfortable rooms in an ivy-clad house overlooking a park by the city walls and windmills. Excellent breakfast with eggs and Belgian chocolate. The best place to stay in this price range. ✚ cll ✉ Oostprootse 14 ☎ 050 33 92 46 🚌 14

DIE SWAENE (€€€)

One of Bruges' most romantic hotels offers 22 beautiful, quiet rooms, some with canal views. Attentive service, and an exceptional restaurant, with a delicious breakfast. ✚ clll ✉ Steenhouwersdijk 1 (Groenerei) ☎ 050 34 27 98; fax 050 33 66 74; www.dieswaene-hotel.com 🚌 1, 6, 11, 16

DUC DE BOURGOGNE (€€)

Slightly aged but comfortable rooms overlooking one of the most picturesque canals. Stylish, traditional restaurant. Just ten rooms—ask for one with a canal view. ✚ blll ✉ Huidenvettersplein 12 ☎ 050 33 20 38; fax 050 344037; www.ducdebourgogne.be 🍴 Dinner daily; lunch Wed–Sun 🚌 1, 6, 11, 16

HOTEL GRAND MIROIR

Brussels' oldest hotel was the Grand Miroir, dating from 1286, on the rue de la Montagne. Guests included Colette, Charles Baudelaire, and Henri de Toulouse-Lautrec, who loved the brothels nearby. The hotel was eventually torn down in the 1950s; the Hotel Metropole carries on in the spirit of the Belle Epoque.

Hotels

GRAND HOTEL DU SABLON (€–€€)

Traditional, city-centre hotel with stained-glass art nouveau dome. The rear part of the hotel was an inn 400 years ago but its 36 pleasant rooms now offer modern facilities.
➕ blll ✉ Noordzandstraat 21 ☎ 050 33 39 02; fax 050 33 39 08; www.sablon.be 🚌 All buses

HOTEL AND PENSION IMPERIAL (€)

Seven pleasantly furnished rooms on a quiet street in the centre of Bruges. The lobby has antiques and bird cages.
➕ blll ✉ 24–28 Dweersstraat ☎ 050 33 90 14; fax 050 34 43 06 🚌 All buses

HOTEL MONTANUS (€€–€€€)

A romantic family-run boutique hotel in a 17th-century mansion with a lovely interior garden. The decor of the 20 rooms is well-chosen modern chic, with a luxury feel.
➕ b–clll ✉ Nieuwe Gentweg 78 ☎ 050 33 84 44; fax 050 34 09 38; www.montanus.be 🚌 1, 11

JACOBS (€)

A friendly, family-run hotel in a quiet location less than ten minutes from the Markt (23 rooms).
➕ clll ✉ Baliestraat 1 ☎ 050 33 98 31; fax 050 33 56 94 🚌 4, 8

MALLEBERG (€–€€)

Well-maintained eight-room hotel in an old house just behind the Burg.
➕ clll ✉ Hoogstraat 7 ☎ 050 34 41 11; fax 050 34 67 69 🚌 All buses to Markt

DE ORANGERIE (€€–€€€)

Nineteen tastefully decorated rooms in a renovated 15th-century convent covered in ivy and overlooking one of Bruges' prettiest corners. In summer, breakfast is served on the terrace by the canal.
➕ blll ✉ Kartuizerinnenstraat 10 ☎ 050 34 16 49; fax 050 33 30 16; www.hotelorangerie.com 🚌 1, 6, 11, 16

PRINSENHOF (€€€)

A quiet and sumptuous 16-room hotel decorated in an elegant traditional Burgundian style with chandeliers, antiques, four-poster beds, and moulded ceilings.
➕ blll ✉ Ontvangersstraat 9 ☎ 050 34 26 90; fax 050 34 23 21; www.prinsenhof.be 🚌 All buses

RELAIS OUD HUIS AMSTERDAM (€€–€€€)

Charming renovation of two 17th-century houses overlooking a quiet canal. The hotel is furnished with antiques, and the 34 rooms are individually decorated.
➕ clll ✉ Spiegelrei 3 ☎ 050 34 18 10; fax 050 33 88 91; www.oha.be 🚌 4, 8

DE TUILERIEEN (€€€)

A 16th-century mansion with views of the Dijver canal and 45 rooms.
➕ blll ✉ Dijver 7 ☎ 050 34 36 91; fax 050 34 04 00; www.hoteltuilerieen.com 🚌 1, 6, 11, 16

BRUSSELS
& BRUGES
travel facts

ESSENTIAL FACTS

Customs regulations

- The guidelines for EU residents (for personal use) are 800 cigarettes, 200 cigars, 1kg tobacco; 10 litres of spirits (over 22 percent), 20 litres of aperitifs, 90 litres of wine, of which 60 can be sparkling wine, 110 litres of beer.
- The limits for non-EU visitors are 200 cigarettes or 50 cigars or 250g of tobacco; 1 litre of spirits (over 22 percent) or 2 litres of fortified wine, 2 litres of still wine; 50g of perfume.
- Visitors under 17 are not entitled to the tobacco and alcohol allowances.

Electricity

- 220v AC. Plugs have two round pins.

Money matters

- Larger shops, hotels, and restaurants accept credit cards.
- Banks exchange money. Out of banking hours, exchange offices operate at Gare du Midi 🕐 7AM–11PM and Gare Centrale 🕐 8AM–9PM. Most banks give cash advances on Eurocard/Mastercard or Visa. Some have offices at the airport.
- The American Express Gold Card Travel Service ✉ 2 place Louise ☎ 02 676 2111 and the American Express Travel & Financial Services ✉ 100 boulevard du Souverain ☎ 02 676 2626; 24-hour Customer Service 02 676 2121 issue traveller's cheques and deal with stolen cards.

Opening hours

- Shops usually open from 9 to 6 or 7. Supermarkets stay open until 9. Many shops in Bruges, fewer in Brussels, close for lunch. The main shopping streets stay open until 9 once a week, usually Friday.
- Banks open at 9 and close between 3.30 and 5; some close for lunch.
- Post offices open from 9 to 5; the main office stays open later.
- Most museums open from 9–4. They generally close on Monday in Brussels, on Tuesday in Bruges. Some close for lunch, and some open longer in the summer. Most museums close at Christmas and some close on public holidays.

Places of Worship

Brussels

- Bruxelles–Acceuil provides times of all the religious services, in all languages ✉ 6 rue de Tabora ☎ 02 511 8178; email bapo@skynet.be.
- Roman Catholic: St. Anne's Church ✉ 10 place de la St.-Alliance ☎ 02 345 5343 🕐 Masses in English Sat 5PM; Sun 10AM and 1PM 🚌 43; St. Nicholas ✉ rue au Beurre ☎ 02 513 8022 🕐 Mass in English Sun 10AM 🚋 Tram 23, 52, 55, 56, 81.
- Anglican: Holy Trinity Church ✉ 29 rue Capitaine ☎ 02 511 7183 🕐 Sun 8.30AM, 10.30AM, 7PM 🚇 Louise/Louiza.
- Jewish: Consistoire Central Israélite de Belgique provides information on Jewish services ✉ rue Joseph Dupont 2 ☎ 02 512 2190.

Bruges

- St. Peter's Chapel ✉ 't Keerske, Keersstraat 1 🕐 English service Sun 6PM 🚌 1, 2, 3, 4, 5, 6, 7, 8, 9, 11, 13, 15, 16, 17, 25.

Public Holidays

- 1 Jan: New Year's Day
  Easter Monday
  1 May: Labour Day
  Ascension Day (sixth Thursday after Easter)
  Whit Monday (seventh Monday after Easter)
  21 Jul: Belgian National Day
  15 Aug: Assumption
  1 Nov: All Saints' Day
  11 Nov: Armistice Day
  25 Dec: Christmas Day.

- If any of these days fall on a Sunday, the following Monday is a holiday.
- The Flemish community also has a holiday on 11 July (Battle of the Golden Spurs), while Walloons (French speaking) have a holiday on 27 September to mark the end of the struggle for independence.

Restrooms

- Public toilets are usually clean. Tip attendants in bigger restaurants and cafés; the amount is posted on the wall.

Smoking

- Smoking is banned in public places, but allowed in restaurants, which rarely have no-smoking areas.

Student travellers

- Reductions are available on ticket prices for all state-run museums for holders of recognized international student cards.

Tourist offices

- The Tourist and Information Office of Brussels (TIB) has maps, brochures, and a hotel reservation service ✉ Town Hall, Grand' Place ☎ 02 513 8940; fax 02 513 8320; www.tib.be 🕓 Daily 9–6 (Sun in winter 10–2).
- Toerisme Vlaanderen (Tourism Flanders) provides information on Bruges and the rest of Flanders ✉ 61 rue du Marché aux Herbe ☎ 02 504 0330; fax 02 504 0270; www.toerismevlaanderen.be 🕓 Jun–Sep: Mon–Fri 9–7; Sat, Sun 9–1, 2–7. Oct–Mar: Mon–Fri 9–6; Sat, Sun 9–1, 2–6.
- Toerisme Brugge ✉ Burg 11, Bruges ☎ 050 44 86 86; fax 050 44 86 00; www.brugge.be 🕓 Oct–Mar: Mon–Fri 9.30–5; Sat, Sun, and hols 9.30–1.15, 2–5.30. Apr–Sep: Mon–Fri 9.30–6.30; Sat, Sun 10–12, 2–6.30.

GETTING ABOUT

Bicycles

- It can be pleasant to cycle in central Brussels, but watch for traffic.
- Travelling around Bruges by bicycle is great. Outside the city, Damme is only 6.5km (4 miles) away, and Knokke or Zeebrugge less than 21km (13 miles).
- Major railway stations sell tickets for train journey and bicycle rental (✉ 02 555 2525). Or try: *Brussels*: Pro Velo ✉ Jul, Aug: rue de l'Infante Isabelle. Sep–Jun: 15 rue de Londres ☎ 02 502 7255
  Bruges: Station Brugge/Bagage ☎ 050 30 23 29
  't Koffieboontje ✉ Hallestraat 4 ☎ 050 33 80 27
  De Ketting ✉ Gentpoortstraat 23 ☎ 050 34 41 96
  Bauhaus Bike Rental ✉ Langestraat 135 ☎ 050 34 10 93.

Buses in Bruges

- Although this guide gives bus numbers for every sight, the city centre is small and it is easy to walk everywhere. However, the efficient bus network makes it easy to explore further afield.
- Buy tickets on board or from newsstands (in which case you must get them stamped on the bus). A one-day pass (*dagticket*) is available.
- Information line ☎ 059 56 53 53.

Buses, trams, and metro in Brussels

- Brussels' metro stations are indicated by a white letter "M".
  Line 1A: Heysel to Hermann Debroux.
  1B: Bizet to Stockel.
  Line 2: Circle line from Simonis to Clémenceau.
  Pré-Métro: from Gare du Nord to Gare du Midi and Albert.

- For information on the metro, trams, and buses in Brussels, contact STIB/MIVB ✉ 6th floor, 20 galerie de la Toison d'Or ☎ General information 02 515 2000; bus information 02 515 3064; www.stib.irisnet.be
- The most economical way to travel is to buy ten tickets (*une carte de dix trajets*), five tickets, or a 12-hour unlimited travel pass. A ticket is valid for one hour on a bus, tram, or metro. You must get the ticket stamped on the bus/tram or in the metro station.
- One-way tickets are available at metro stations, from bus or tram drivers, or at newsagents with the STIB sign. Special tickets are available at metro stations or from the Tourist Office in Grand' Place.
- A one-day Tourist Passport, available from the tourist office on Grand' Place, also includes reductions on admission to museums.

Maps

- In Brussels, street names and some metro stations are marked in French and Flemish. In Bruges only Flemish is used. Pick up free bus and metro maps and time-tables from tourist offices, the metro, the STIB/MIVB office in the Gare du Midi station, and the bus office at Bruges railway station.

Taxis

- In Brussels, use only official taxis, with a taxi light on the roof. Taxis are metered and can be called or flagged down. Drivers are not allowed to stop if you are less than 100m (110 yards) from a taxi stand. The meter price is per kilometre and is doubled if you travel outside the city ☎ 02 268 0000 or 02 349 4343.
- In Bruges, taxi stands are on Markt ☎ 050 33 44 44 and at the railway station ☎ 050 38 46 60.

Trains

- Brussels has three main stations: Gare du Midi/Zuidstation, Gare Centrale/Centraal Station, and Gare du Nord/Noordstation. Two other stations, Schumann and Quartier Léopold, serve the EU institutions, and the headquarters of NATO. Bruges has only one station near the city centre.
- Tickets are sold in stations, not on the train. Special offers are available on weekends and for day trips.
- Frequent trains from Brussels centre run to the outlying areas and from Bruges to the coast.
- Train information: SNCB/NMBS Brussels ☎ 02 555 2525 or for Bruges ☎ 050 38 23 82.

MEDIA & COMMUNICATIONS

Mail

- Stamps are available from post offices and vending machines.
- Central Post Office ✉ 1E/F avenue Fosny, next to the Gare du Midi in Brussels ☎ 02 538 3398 ⏰ 24 hours
- Bruges post office ✉ Markt 5 ☎ 050 33 14 11 ⏰ Mon–Fri 9.30–5; Sat 9.30–1.

Newspapers

- Belgian papers include the Flemish *De Morgen* and *De Standaard*, and the French *Le Soir*.

Telephones

- Many phone booths accept only prepaid phone cards, available from post offices, supermarkets, stations, and newsstands.
- International calls are expensive. Rates are slightly lower 8PM–8AM and on Sundays and holidays.
- The city codes (02 for Brussels; 050 for Bruges) must be used even when calling from within the city.
- To call the UK from Belgium dial 00 44, then drop the first 0 from

the area code. To call Belgium from the UK dial 00 32, then drop the first 0 from the area code.

- To call the US from Belgium dial 001. To call Belgium from the US dial 011 32, then drop the first 0 from the area code.

EMERGENCIES

Emergency phone numbers
- Ambulance/fire ☎ 100
- Police ☎ 101
- Brussels doctors on emergency call ☎ 02 479 1818
- Bruges doctors on emergency call ⊙ Fri–Mon 8AM–8PM ☎ 050 81 38 99

Embassies and consulates
Brussels
- Canada ✉ 2 ave de Tervuren ☎ 02 741 0611
- Ireland ✉ 189 rue Froissart ☎ 02 230 5337
- UK ✉ 85 rue d'Arlon ☎ 02 287 6211
- US ✉ 25–27 boulevard du Régent ☎ 02 508 2111

Lost Property
- Report lost property to the police. For insurance purposes, always ask for a certificate of loss.
- Central police station, Brussels ✉ rue du Marché au Charbon ☎ 02 517 9611
- Lost Property on the metro or buses ✉ Inside Porte de Namur metro station next to Press Shop, Brussels ☎ 02 515 2394; ✉ Hauwerstraat 7, Bruges ☎ 050 44 88 44

Medical treatment
- ▶ 6 for details of E111 form.
- Standards of medical care are high. Most doctors speak French and English. Doctors see patients at their offices, but will visit if you are too sick to move. Visits must be paid for in cash or by cheque. The following hospitals provide 24-hour emergency assistance:

Brussels
- Hôpital Universitaire St-Luc ✉ 10 avenue d'Hippocrate ☎ 02 764 1111
- Hôpital St-Pierre ✉ 322 rue Haute ☎ 02 535 3111
- Hôpital Universitaire des Enfants Reine Fabiola (paediatric) ✉ 15 avenue Jean Cocq ☎ 02 477 3100

Bruges
- Algemeen Ziekenhuis Sint-Jan Te Brugge ✉ Ruddershave 10 ☎ 050 45 21 11
- Algemeen Ziekenhuis Sint-Lucas ✉ Campus St-Lucas, St-Lucaslaan 29 ☎ 050 36 91 11

Medicines
- Pharmacies (*Pharmacie/Apotheek*), marked with a green cross, open Mon–Fri 9–6. Each displays a list of pharmacies that open outside these hours.

Sensible precautions
- By law, visitors over 21 must carry a passport or ID card at all times.
- Watch out for pickpockets and bag-snatchers in the crowded areas of Brussels and around stations.
- In Brussels, take a taxi at night, rather than the metro, bus, or tram.
- Belgium in general is as safe as other parts of Europe. Be careful in downtown Brussels, especially the red-light area at Gare du Nord, which can be dangerous at night, and the area around the Comte de Flandre metro station, which is known for street crime.

LANGUAGE

- It is often easier to speak English, which is widely understood: If you speak French to a Flemish person, they might be offended. Similarly, if you speak Flemish to a French-speaking *Bruxellois* they may well reply in French with some disdain.

Index

Citypack
Brussels & Bruges

AUTHORS AND EDITION REVISERS *Anthony Sattin and Sylvie Franquet*
COVER DESIGN *Tigist Getachew, Fabrizio La Rocca*

ISBN 1–4000–1226–0

SECOND EDITION

ACKNOWLEDGMENTS
The authors would like to thank Nica and Willy Brouke-Diercx, Mr Drubble of the Bruges Tourist
Office, Moeke and Leo Franquet, Pauline Owen and the Belgian Tourist Office, London, Jim Rowe
and Eurostar, Irene Rossi, M. Serge Schultz of Hotel Metropole, Frank Vanderlinden, and the many
organisations who made their research a pleasure.
The Automobile Association would like to thank the following photographers, libraries and
associations for their assistance in the preparation of this book.
BRIDGEMAN ART LIBRARY 16r Town Plan of Bruges, from 'Civitates Orbis Terrarum' by Goerg
Braun (1541–1622) and Frans Hogenburh (1535–90), c. 1572 (coloured engraving) by Joris
Hoefnagel (1542–1600) (after); Private Collection; GROENINGEMUSEUM 47t, 47b; MARY EVANS
PICTURE LIBRARY 16l, 16r, 17r; MEMLING MUSEUM 44b; MUSÉE D'ART MODERNE 33;
SPECTRUM COLOUR LIBRARY 61, 89b; STOCKBYTE 5; www.euro.ecb.int/ 6 (euro notes).
The remaining pictures are held in the Association's own library (AA PHOTO LIBRARY) and were
taken by Alex Kouprianoff.

IMPORTANT TIP
Time inevitably brings changes, so always confirm prices, travel facts, and other perishable
information when it matters. Although Fodor's cannot accept responsibility for errors, you
can use this guide in the confidence that we have taken every care to ensure its accuracy.

SPECIAL SALES
Fodor's Travel Publications are available at special discounts for bulk purchases
(100 copies or more) for sales promotions or premiums. Special editions, including
personalized covers, excerpts of existing guides, and corporate imprints, can be created in
large quantities for special needs. For more information contact your local bookseller or
write to Special Marketing, Fodor's Travel Publications, 1745 Broadway, New York, NY
10019. Inquiries from Canada should be directed to your local Canadian bookseller or sent
to Random House of Canada, Ltd., Marketing Department, 2775 Matheson Blvd. East,
Mississauga, Ontario L4W 4P7.

Colour separation by Daylight Colour Art Pte Ltd, Singapore
Manufactured by Dai Nippon Printing Co. (Hong Kong) Ltd
10 9 8 7 6 5 4 3 2 1

A01084
Fold out map © Mairs Geographischer Verlag / Falk Verlag, 73751 Ostfildern
Transport map © TCS, Aldershot, England

TITLES IN THE CITYPACK SERIES
• Amsterdam • Bangkok • Barcelona • Beijing • Berlin • Boston • Brussels & Bruges •
• Chicago • Dublin • Florence • Hong Kong • Lisbon • London • Los Angeles •
• Madrid • Melbourne • Miami • Montreal • Munich • New York City • Paris • Prague •
• Rome • San Francisco • Seattle • Shanghai • Singapore • Sydney • Tokyo • Toronto •
• Venice • Vienna • Washington, D.C. •